PELICAN BOOK A839
THE ARCHITECT AND SOCIETY
Edited by John Fleming and Hugh Honour

Inigo Jones

Sir John Summerson, who has been curator of Sir John Soane's Museum since 1945, was knighted in 1958. Born in 1904, he was educated at Harrow and University College, London. After working in architects' offices he became an architectural instructor at the Edinburgh College of Art in 1929. From 1934 until 1941 he was assistant editor of *The Architect and Building News,* and then for the next four years deputy director of the National Buildings Record. After the war he was a lecturer in the history of architecture at the Architectural Association and at Birkbeck College, University of London. In 1958-9 he lectured as Slade Professor of Fine Art at Oxford and he was elected to the Slade chair at Cambridge in 1966. He serves or has served on a number of commissions, including the Royal Fine Art Commission, the Royal Commission on Historical Monuments, and the Historical Manuscripts Commission. He has been chairman of the National Council for Diplomas in Art and Design since 1961. Among his publications are works on Nash, Ben Nicholson (in Penguin Modern Painters), Sir John Soane and Wren, and he is also author of *Architecture in Britain 1530–1830* in the Pelican History of Art. His most recent work is *The Book of Architecture of John Thorpe,* an analytical catalogue compiled for the Walpole Society. Sir John Summerson, who is married and has three sons, lives in Hampstead.

Inigo Jones

by John Summerson

PENGUIN BOOKS

Penguin Books Ltd, Harmondsworth,
Middlesex, England
Penguin Books Inc., 3300 Clipper Mill Road,
Baltimore 11, Md, U.S.A.
Penguin Books Australia Ltd, Ringwood,
Victoria, Australia

First published 1966
Copyright © John Summerson, 1966

Designed by Gerald Cinamon
Made and printed in Great Britain by
Balding and Mansell, London and Wisbech
Set in Monotype Garamond

Contents

Acknowledgements

Her Majesty the Queen graciously permitted the photograph of the interior of the Queen's Chapel, St James's, to be taken for this book. The guardians of the three great collections of Inigo Jones drawings – the Trustees of the Chatsworth Settlement, the Royal Institute of British Architects and the Provost and Fellows of Worcester College, Oxford – have kindly allowed me to reproduce drawings in their collections. The location of each drawing is indicated at the end of the list which follows. Those attributed to the RIBA form part of the Burlington–Devonshire collection, on permanent loan to the library and the Institute.

Illustrations

Illustration Credits

Inigo Jones

1. Sir Anthony Van Dyck. Portrait of Inigo Jones

Introduction

Inigo Jones was the first English classical architect; he was also the post-humous sponsor of the Palladian movement of the eighteenth century. But the obvious magnitude of his claim as founder and progenitor has, for the last two hundred years, diverted attention from the actual nature of his own art. It has become easier to see Jones as the source of someone else's artistic enterprise than to see Jones as Jones. If we try for a moment to forget that he was 'the first' in this issue or that, that it was his 'influence' which had this or that effect, if we try to enclose him in his own time and look into his works instead of outward from them, we find ourselves gazing at something extremely hard to bring into focus.

For this, there is one terribly clear reason. Out of forty-five recorded architectural works of Inigo Jones, only *seven* survive. Of the remaining thirty-eight there exist utterly inadequate records and in some instances none. Then again, the figure of Jones is obscured by such a swarm of misattributions that the toil of discernment enfeebles perception; and, what is worse, some of these misattributions are by now so old and so respectable that their influence on the Jonesian image is all but inde-structible. The task of piecing together the verifiably authentic remains and reconstructing them into something recognizable as part of a once consistent whole is not promising. It is, nevertheless, worth attempting and what follows here is a study towards this end.

First there are some fundamental biographical questions to be asked, and answered as best we can. Where did Inigo Jones come from? When and under what circumstances did he become an architect?

Early Years

Inigo Jones was baptized on 19 July 1573 in the church of St Bartholomew-the-Less, Smithfield. His father was also called Inigo, an otherwise un-heard-of name which the son sometimes latinized as Ignatius but which is almost certainly Welsh. He was a clothworker. He died in 1597 and his will shows that he had, besides Inigo, three daughters – Joan, Judith and Mary. Inigo proved the will on 5 April of that year when he was twenty-three. The father was not rich.

The only evidence we have about Inigo's youth is that a Dr Harwood told George Vertue, the antiquary, that he had it from Sir Christopher Wren that Inigo was apprenticed to a joiner in St Paul's Churchyard. If he was apprenticed at fourteen, the year would be 1587–8 and he would be out of his articles in 1594–5. This is a quite likely beginning for a young man of obvious artistic talents; some Elizabethan joiners in London handled a great variety of designing and craftsmanship. But it is not till eight years later, in 1603, that we first hear of Inigo Jones as a professional man – and the profession is that of 'picture-maker'. This term was begin-ning to be used to distinguish between painters whose business it was to lay colours on parts of buildings and those who painted pictorial compositions. Inigo was one of these and he was paid ten pounds for his services as such by the Earl of Rutland. The great biographical question is, what was he doing between the date at which he proved his father's will (1597) and that of his first recorded professional earnings in 1603? How did he become a picture-maker?

Our only guide at this stage is John Webb, Inigo's pupil and a relation by marriage, who compiled, after Inigo's death, a book on Stonehenge, written as if by his master but confessedly manufactured by Webb on the basis of 'some few indigested notes'. At the beginning he makes Jones say: 'Being naturally inclined in my younger years to study the Arts of Design,

I passed into foreign parts to converse with the great masters thereof in Italy.' The first part of this sentence deliberately echoes the first words of Palladio's introduction to his famous treatise *I quattro libri dell'architettura*: '*Da naturale inclinatione guidato mi diedi ne i miei primi anni allo studio dell'Architettura.*' But it is to be noted that instead of 'architecture' Webb puts 'arts of design'; from which we may infer that architecture was not Inigo's main interest when he first went abroad and that he was preparing to be a 'picture-maker'. This is borne out by various factors in his subsequent history.

These early travels are obscure. John Webb, in a sequel to the Stonehenge book, tells us that his first royal patron was Christian IV of Denmark whom Webb speaks of as 'sending for him out of Italy, where especially at Venice, he had many years resided'. Christian IV's sister Anne was James I's queen. Inigo, according to Webb, crossed over to England with King Christian when he paid his first visit to the English court, and forthwith entered the service of Queen Anne. Actually, Inigo must have come over at least a year before the Danish king, whose first visit to England was in 1606. He had already been engaged on a masque for the Queen in 1605.

But the main question concerns Italy. Inigo certainly must have been there between his father's death in 1597 and the payment to him by the Earl of Rutland in 1603. A slightly dubious clue is a worn inscription with the date 1601 on a fly-leaf of his annotated copy of Palladio. That he was mostly in Venice we need not doubt, but how he got there, at whose expense and in what company is unknown. An Englishman who would be in Venice at about the same time was Henry Wotton (the future ambassador), who had left England apparently in order to avoid involvement in the troubles descending on the Earl of Essex, whose secretary he had been. At a later date Wotton shared Jones's interest in Palladio and possessed some of the master's original drawings. An association with Jones at the earlier period, not only in Venice but in the circle of the Earl of Essex, is not impossible.

But Venice, though obviously of great importance to Jones, does not supply the courtly pattern which his own career was to follow. That is more probably to be found in Florence. There, the Medici court under Ferdinand i was one of the most decorative and artistically productive in Europe. The court entertainments were the source of the masque in its most ambitious forms and Jones must certainly have had deep acquaintance with the masques produced at the Palazzo Pitti and the Palazzo Vecchio. At the head of the artistic life of Florence was the architect (who was also painter and sculptor) Bernardo Buontalenti; his abilities were large – they ranged from the planning of Leghorn, through the conception of monumental buildings like the Logge dei Banchi at Pisa, to the design of objects to be produced in the court porcelain factory. He created the grotto in the Boboli gardens. He designed scenery and costumes for the masques. In short, he occupied at the Medici court very much the position of general artistic authority that Inigo Jones was to occupy later at those of James i and Charles i. If we want to see Jones's career in a European perspective, this Florentine adumbration helps.

Webb implies that Jones's period in Italy came to an end when the King of Denmark, the first of his five royal masters, 'engross'd Him to himself, sending for Him out of Italy'. Christian iv at this time was still in his twenties – an expansive, jubilant young monarch, ready to buy foreign genius for his court whether in the shape of Dutchmen to conduct his fortification works or Flemings for his architectural enterprises. To bring an Englishman out of Italy to work in Denmark seems a rather odd proceeding, but Webb assures us that Jones's reputation in Italy was altogether extraordinary for a northerner. Besides, the 'sending for him' may not have been quite as peremptory as it sounds. Jones, after all, was not a Danish subject. It happens, furthermore, that in the year that the Earl of

Rutland remunerated him as a 'picture-maker', the Earl was about to lead an embassy to Denmark, bearing the order of the Garter to King Christian on the occasion of the christening of his first son. Jones may have accompanied this embassy. If he did and if he had only lately returned to England from Italy, the evidence allows six years for his Italian residence, justifying the 'many years' of Webb's account. It means, however, that Jones, leaving for Denmark in 1603, would be in the Danish king's service for only a year, since, as we have seen, he produced his first masque for the King's sister in January 1605.

Jones's international reputation is something upon which Webb insists with great vehemence. He was 'the *Vitruvius* of his age', he says in one place and, elsewhere, 'it was *Vox Europae* that named him so, being, much more than at home, famous in remote parts, where he lived many years, designed many works, and discovered many antiquities, before unknown, with general Applause'. This is a vast claim and no evidence has ever been found to substantiate it. There are, indeed, two curious traditions. One is that he designed the church in the Piazza at Leghorn. This, built in 1581-95, is known to be the work of Pieroni, following Buontalenti, and if the tradition is not pure fabrication (traditions rarely are) it can only mean that some minor connexion with the work became enlarged into the act of designing when Jones's own equivalent to Leghorn came before the world at Covent Garden. The other tradition is that he designed the Börs or Exchange at Copenhagen. This is more easily explained. The Exchange was begun in 1619 by Laurens Steenwinkel in an elaborate Flemish style. Its general form, however, was probably suggested by the New Exchange built in the Strand, London, in 1608. For that building, as we shall see, Inigo certainly supplied a design. That Christian IV should obtain a copy of it for his own architects to consult is more likely than not.

From 1605, when he was thirty-two and certainly in England, Inigo Jones's career becomes easier to follow. He was still, so far as we can ascertain, a painter and decorative artist rather than an architect. Not a single painting attributable to him with certainty is known. We have, however, some drawings. One, of a tabernacle sheltering an enthroned monarch, is perhaps the earliest. Then we have four costume designs for a masque which was performed in 1605; and eight for another in 1606. These are the earliest Inigo drawings known to exist. The first architectural drawings belong to about 1608 and, though delicately drawn, are so amateurish in technique as to suggest that their author had only just turned his attention to the subject. It was as a 'picture-maker' and as a designer in a very general and mostly non-architectural sense that Inigo entered the service of the English court.

The Masques

In England 'Queen Ann', says Webb, 'honoured Him with her service first'. The Queen, crowned at Windsor with her husband in 1603, took up residence in London in the following year and threw herself into the promotion of court entertainments. She was the patroness of many of the early masques, of those who wrote them and of Inigo Jones who, more often than not, devised the scenes and costumes. The first of the Queen's masques was the *Masque of Blackness*, a piece in which twelve daughters of Niger, in a dialogue between Niger, Oceanus and Aethiopia, are introduced, for the sake of their complexions, to Albion. This was written by Ben Jonson and performed in the old Banqueting House at Whitehall on Twelfth Night (6 January) 1605. The second masque patronized by the Queen and written by Jonson was the *Masque of Beauty*. In this the daughters of Niger, their number increased by four, again appeared, this time in a mobile temple. The performance was the first in a new (but still not the present) Banqueting House and took place on Twelfth Night 1608. In the intervening years, 1606 and 1607, there were masques patronized by the King, and Jones designed at least one of them. Then, in 1609, came the *Masque of Queens*, in 1610 *Tethys' Festival* [2] and in 1611 *Love Freed from Ignorance*, all initiated by the Queen and all designed by Jones. By the time of the last, however, he had been appointed Surveyor to Prince Henry; nor does the Queen seem to have taken the initiative in any further court entertainments.

These early masques were, for England, a wonderful innovation. They introduced something resembling the *intermezzo*, which at the Medici court had developed from small beginnings as an entr'acte into a dramatic species of its own – a species in which poetry, movement and scenic devices combined to set intensely in relief a theme rooted in classical mythology but conveying sentiments appropriate to contemporary occasions. In Ben Jonson's hands there was nothing trivial about these masques. They were short, but highly wrought in every dimension. The texts were distillations of immense learning and models of literary craftsmanship; they were long in preparation and extremely expensive, often costing as much as it would take to build a fair-sized country house; and the costumes, lighting and contrivances may, at their best (it is impossible on the evidence to be sure) have begotten true theatrical magic.

The conception, general shape and spoken lines of each masque were the work of a man of letters – most often Ben Jonson but sometimes Daniel, Campion or Chapman or, in later years, Townsend or d'Avenant. The actual visual images, the transformations and illusionist effects were the work of an artist-technician – nearly always Jones. Over 450 drawings by him for this kind of work survive at Chatsworth, representing work on twenty-five masques, a pastoral and two plays, and ranging in date between 1605 and 1641. They go very little way towards giving us an idea of the total effect of any one production. Nor do they go far in explaining the mechanical side – the motivated billows of *Blackness*, the dividing rocks in *Hue and Cry* or the disappearing Hell in the *Masque of Beauty*. What they do show us is Jones's quality as an Italian-trained draughtsman, not only in the charming if somewhat repetitive costume designs but in scenes of romantic landscape and sometimes fantasic, sometimes classical architecture. Not all are equally striking as inventions. Among the later designs are some which are mere paraphrases of known Italian originals.

From 1605 till 1611 Jones probably regarded himself as primarily under the Queen's protection though at the service of the sovereign himself when required and of others as occasion might arise. It was during this period that he first turned to architecture.

2. Tethys, a nymph. Design for *Tethys' Festival*, 1610

3. A nymph. Design for *Chloridia*, 1631

The First Architectural Designs

'Architecture', in the England of this time, was a rare word, at once invoking *architectura*, the Roman science of building. 'Architect' was no more common and was a rather grandiose and literary appellation for somebody who designed buildings. Nearly all the building work of James I's reign was designed by those who built it, and they were masons, bricklayers or carpenters, working in with other trades which might include carvers for exterior ornament and joiners and plasterers for interiors. These were the people who built the kind of buildings which we naturally call 'Jacobean', which is to say gabled buildings with mullioned windows still substantially in the medieval tradition but modified by successive waves of fashion through the reigns of the Tudors. Rather apart from these building craftsmen, however, was a class of men calling themselves 'surveyors'. The Latin equivalent is *supervisor*, which indicates a managing superiority to the artisan. The surveyors of Tudor times were mostly concerned with land and came into prominence and prosperity with the agrarian revolution; but they also claimed management skill in building and were, in fact, the prototypes of the modern professional architect.

At the time when Inigo Jones first turned his attention to architecture many surveyors with strong architectural inclinations were at work in and outside London. The most consequential, by virtue of his office, was Simon Basil, Surveyor of the King's Works, whom we shall meet later because Jones succeeded him. There was Robert Stickells whom the editors of Stow's *Chronicle* (1631) describe as 'The excellent Artichect of our time'. There was John Thorpe who designed houses for the newly rich in Kensington and left a wonderful collection of plans, now in the Soane Museum. There was Robert Lyming who designed most of Hatfield. In the midlands there was the great Robert Smythson, creator of Wollaton and Hardwick. These men came, for the most part, out of the building trades, but could draw and write well and often knew some Latin. Their culture was, however, strictly limited; they rarely travelled abroad and possessed no intellectual authority. The role of the designer as a man of intellectual status was left for Jones.

In the library of Worcester College, Oxford, are two drawings which almost certainly belong to the year 1608. One of them is a design for the street elevation of the New Exchange [4] in the Strand. This building represented a personal venture by the Lord Treasurer, the Earl of Salisbury, on the lines of Gresham's Royal Exchange in the City. He had acquired part of the site of Durham House and the first stone of the new building was laid on 10 June 1608. As built, it differed much from Jones's design and may or may not have been his work. But the design itself, certainly by him, is of great interest. Delicately drawn and coloured, it is nevertheless obviously the work of somebody who had had little to do with architecture and nothing with building. Many of its elements are traceable to engravings in Serlio and Palladio, and the lower part is a more or less orthodox classical arcade. The three towers riding on pediments, however, and the huge scrolls in the centrepiece supporting monstrous candelabra, are the kind of thing which might do well enough in a scene

4. Design for the New Exchange in the Strand, c.1608

for a masque but are unrealizable in building terms. As evidence of the date at which Jones turned his attention to architecture the drawing is eloquent. On the one hand, he is totally inexperienced. On the other, his intentions are serious and ambitious. He turns his back on the English vernacular and sets his face towards Italian authority.

The second drawing at Worcester College is no less curious and instructive. It shows the thirteenth-century tower of old St Paul's Cathedral [5] surmounted by a new arcade and, above this, an octagonal dome of

5. Design for the completion of the central tower, old St Paul's Cathedral, c.1608

ogee profile terminating in a balustraded gallery and short conical spire. At each corner of the tower is a similar spire. The occasion for this design was probably James I's approach to the Lord Mayor and Bishop of London in July 1608, requiring them to have the Cathedral surveyed and to obtain estimates for its repair and for a new spire. The old spire had been struck by lightning nearly fifty years before and never restored. There was no special reason why Inigo Jones should design the new spire, except indeed his rising fame at court and, most probably, the patronage of the Earl of Salisbury who, as we have seen, had employed him on the New Exchange. Salisbury was behind the St Paul's project.

This is a very queer design. The arcaded stage is a feeble imitation of the arcades in the Basilica Palladiana at Vicenza; the spire and pinnacles are incongruously collected from Labacco's illustration of Sangallo's design for St Peter's; the dome, presumably a concession to Tudor tradition but with the curvature of a classical scroll, comes awkwardly over the arcades, with four of its eight edges standing on them and four sidling off behind the pinnacles. Both architecturally and structurally the design is a beginner's – a fact which the neat draughtsmanship and colouring do nothing to disguise.

At the RIBA is another St Paul's design – for a new west front [43, p. 100]. In part, it is a paraphrase of the façade of the Gesù church in Rome, but there are features resembling the New Exchange design and it almost certainly belongs to the same year, 1608. The architecture is perhaps a little more skilful and the sculpture is well drawn. But rusticated masonry (so important in Jones's later work) is used without understanding. Again, this is backcloth architecture.

This paper evidence provides us with secure knowledge of Inigo's degree of skill in architecture around 1608. His architectural ambitions may go back a little earlier. A Latin dedication in a book given to him by Edmund Bolton, the Cambridge scholar, at the end of 1606, is to Inigo

Jones 'through whom there is hope that sculpture, modelling, architecture, painting, acting and all that is praise-worthy in the elegant arts of the ancients, may one day find their way across the Alps into our England'. It happens that earlier in the same year a building in which all those arts had a part to play had been begun in Whitehall – a new Banqueting House, of brick and timber, built on the site of its decrepit Elizabethan predecessor and built, we may surmise, to accommodate the new style of masque which Ben Jonson and Jones had lately introduced. This building, finished in 1609, had a life of only eleven years, being burnt down in 1619; but we know enough about it to be sure that the interior, at least, was classical. It had galleries with Doric order below and Ionic above, on the lines of a Vitruvian basilica or 'Egyptian' hall. This is what one would expect from Jones (and nobody else that we know of) and, furthermore, it is in principle the type of interior which Jones adopted in his great new Banqueting House of 1619-22 – the one which still stands. He was, in fact, almost certainly the architect.

It was unfortunate that when this Banqueting House was half built, James I took a dislike to the way the columns obstructed the light. But the cloud passed and Jones's reputation continued to rise. He had the patronage of the Lord Treasurer who was building his new house at Hatfield, the great arcaded gallery of which (dated 1611) ornately imitates Jones's design for the New Exchange. In 1609 he was employed to carry letters to France and took the opportunity of seeing, among other things, Paris and Chambord. In 1610 he was given the enviable appointment of Surveyor to the heir to the throne – Henry, Prince of Wales.

Surveyor to Prince Henry

Invested at the age of sixteen, in May 1610, the Prince of Wales held his court at St James's Palace. It was an establishment of inordinate size reproducing many of the offices of the Whitehall court with, perhaps, more regard to tradition than to usefulness. It became at once a magnet for ambitious talent. Henry was looked to as a model prince, the 'universal man' of Renaissance philosophy, a leader and patron equally in the active and contemplative arts. The appointment of Jones, the only Renaissance architect in England, seems in the perspective of history exactly right; and so, doubtless, it seemed to Jones. So it might have proved, had not the Prince succumbed to typhoid fever in September 1612. The thronged, hopeful court of St James's and Richmond had lasted barely two and a half years.

Jones's association with Prince Henry left little mark. In January 1610, he designed the setting and costumes for *Prince Henries Barriers*, a dramatic tourney with speeches from King Arthur, Merlin and the Lady of the Lake, written by Ben Jonson; but none of the designs survives. At the same time, St James's Palace began to receive the proper equipment for a Prince who was also a student and collector. Jones may have been responsible for the elaborate library interior, for wainscoting the Long Gallery to receive the Prince's pictures and for arbours in the Privy Garden, but we cannot be sure. These things were all paid for through the King's Works. The Prince's own office of works, with Jones at its head, seems to have achieved nothing specific and there is a hint in one of the accounts that the overlapping of the two offices in the works at Richmond Palace merely caused confusion. Probably the happiest creation resulting from Prince Henry's patronage of Jones was the masque, *Oberon*, performed on 1 January 1611, and containing an absurd and delightful romantic palace, the design for which survives at Chatsworth [6]. This nonsense-architecture has some

6. Oberon's Palace. Design for *Oberon*, 1610

7. (*Opposite*) Newmarket. Design for a stable, 1617

relation to whatever is nonsense in the New Exchange design, but here, in the proper dominion of nonsense, there is nothing to reproach.

Even had Prince Henry lived it is rather doubtful if his Surveyor would have enjoyed any special architectural opportunities. The young man's taste was for grandiose water-works and grotesque devices, rather than the calculated harmonies of classicism, and in these thing he was well served by two foreigners – the Frenchman, Salamon de Caux, and an Italian from the Medici court, Constantino de Servi. De Servi, indeed, seems to have made so much headway with the Prince as to threaten Jones's authority altogether.

Mourning for the Prince lasted no great time, because the King's daughter, the Princess Elizabeth, betrothed to the Prince Palatine, heir to the throne of Bohemia, was to be married in February. Arrangements were already in hand. They included two great masques. The *Lords Masque*, written by Thomas Campion, was performed on the marriage night itself, 14 February 1613, in the Banqueting House. *The Masque of the Inns of Court*,

written by George Chapman, was performed on the night following in the Great Hall. Inigo Jones designed them both. Of his designs for the first, four splendid costume drawings survive: but of the scene itself nothing; which is tantalizing, for Campion, in his introduction to the printed version, praises the architecture of the occasion, with its golden, gem-studded pilasters, its capitals 'composed and of a new invention' and its upper 'bastard order with Cartouses reversed, comming from the Capitals of every Pillaster . . . rich and full of ornament'. Chapman's masque is as lacking in architectural evidence, but architecture there probably was, for Chapman accords his friend Inigo the title of 'our Kingdome's most Art-full and Ingenious Architect'.

These masques set the seal on Jones's reputation. He was now, at forty, a great man: the pre-eminent authority at court on all matters of art and design. His advancement to high office in an appropriate sphere was predictable, and on 27 April he was granted the reversion of the place of Surveyor of the King's Works. On that particular date, however, Jones was probably abroad.

ιe Second Italian Journey

es's second Italian visit was made under radiant auspices. Thomas
ward, second Earl of Arundel, destined to be one of the greatest of
lish patrons and art collectors, was at this time twenty-seven. He had
ι one of the outstanding figures in Prince Henry's circle; he was a
ιd of Jones and had taken part, with his wife, in several of his masques.
ν he was deputed by the King to be one of the noblemen to escort the
ιce Palatine and his bride to their home at Heidelberg. He chose to
ιe this formal journey as the first stage of a much longer but less formal
, indeed, almost clandestine one, amounting to a long sight-seeing
:grination through the cities of Italy. For this, he attached Jones to his
ε: few Englishmen of the time will have known Italy so well and none
ntiquities with such authority.

he party left London on 18 April and reached Heidelberg on 7 June. A
k later, Arundel and his suite left Heidelberg, travelling by way of
sbourg and Basle to Milan, thence to Parma and Venice. At Venice
Earl was entertained in state. He was there for the first fortnight of
tember. Then his travels took on a more private character and he must
e leaned much on Jones's advice. He returned to Padua and after
:ing Vicenza and Bologna went to Florence, then Siena. The winter of
ʒ-14 was spent in Rome. Here Arundel obtained permission to ex-
ιte an ancient site and was able to send some statues back to England.
m Rome the party moved to Naples, was probably back in Rome in
ʳ and June but spent most of the summer of 1614 at Genoa. In Septem-
they travelled north, returning to England by way of Turin and Paris.
ɛ tour had lasted one year and seven months.

ιigo Jones's movements in relation to those of the Earl and his party
ιncertain, but it is obvious that he had plenty of liberty and used it to
:tise himself in Italian art and architecture. At Chatsworth is a book

filled, in the course of 1614, with sketches and observations. He was still a 'picture-maker' and Italian painting absorbed him. He collected engravings and copied from them, *per pratica,* as he says, into his sketchbook. Among the older painters the one who interested him most, apart from the obvious classics, was Parmigianino, while among living painters there was the young Guercino whom Jones met and whose style of draughtsmanship decisively influenced his own. In architecture he took for his guide Palladio's treatise, the *Quattro libri dell'architettura,* visiting as many as possible of the buildings illustrated in it and conning them over, line by line, against Palladio's woodcuts. His annotated Palladio survives at Worcester College. It was of great importance to him; but it was not the only book and too much is sometimes made of Jones's dependence on Palladio. The fact is that he absorbed at least as much from Serlio and something from Labacco. Scamozzi he met in Venice. That master's great *Idea dell'Architettura universale* had not yet appeared but when it reached Jones in England it had as profound an effect on his designs as Palladio. Jones was interested not so much in this or that personality in Italian architecture, still less in anybody's personal style. He was interested basically in the *antique* and all that Vitruvius had to say about it; and after that in the whole fabric of Italian theory from Alberti onwards, even as far as Zanini, his own contemporary, whose book appeared in 1629. Nor did he overlook the greatest of French theorists, Philibert de l'Orme. Furthermore, Jones had not merely a technical and emotional but a philosophical interest in architecture, as we may see from the books he possessed, the passages he underlined and the marginal notes he made. If Jones, returning from Italy in 1615, had brought with him merely the infection of an Italian manner and cultivated it as his own he might have done very well; but he would have been provincial. Provincial is exactly what Jones was not. If the architecture he eventually built in England had been built in Italy it would have been against the tide – an individual radicalism.

Jones's second visit to Italy confirmed him as an architect. He had before him the prospect of the Surveyorship and, as a preparation for this, the golden experience which Arundel's wealth and interest had provided. Simon Basil, the Surveyor in office, was, it is true, still alive and active. Had he remained so, Jones might have been joined with him in the convenient fashion often adopted in the King's service. But it so happened that, in September 1615, Basil died.

The Surveyor

It was a very long time since a man of such eminence as Inigo Jones had occupied the Surveyorship of the King's Works – not, indeed, since Sir Richard Lee, Henry VIII's great military engineer. The Elizabethan Surveyors had been of small account. The most distinguished of them was Robert Adams, a fortifications expert and notable draughtsman. Simon Basil's chief asset was having been Adams's right-hand man, his only other the patronage of the Cecils.

Queen Elizabeth had built almost nothing; in her reign the Office of Works had been a mere palace maintenance department, running on a budget of no more than £4,000 a year. James I soon changed that. In eighteen months in 1607-9 his Works disposed of £23,000 and in the following eighteen months of over £50,000. When Inigo Jones took office the tide of Royal building was flowing extravagantly – it was a great moment to be Britain's first architect. What Leonardo had been to the Sforzas, Giulio Romano to the Gonzagas and, in latter years, Buontalenti to the Medicis it now seemed Jones's role and opportunity to be to the Stuarts.

Not that the Surveyorship was an office entailing merely or principally artistic creation and promotion. Indeed, in the official documents which reflect the history of the Works organization, questions of 'art' have scarcely any place at all. Jones's principal function was as chairman of a board of administrators and artisans whose business was to keep in suitable repair the 'houses of access' in current use by the sovereign and his consort and to ensure their comfort and safety in any house where they might be. The board retained a staff of clerks-of-works and engaged outside contractors on task-work. It obtained its funds from the Exchequer through warrants under the Privy Seal, distributed them throughout the various undertakings, and declared annually an audited statement of accounts before the Lord Treasurer. If most of this business was delegated to the Comptroller, Paymaster, artisans and clerks, the Surveyor still had an unremitting stream of crude business to attend to. Under James I and Charles I one of the heaviest burdens was the enforcement of the Proclamations concerning the increase of building in London. Evasions had to be examined and brought to book. So had nuisances and encroachments of various kinds and infringements of regulations regarding building materials. In the Domestic State Papers, references to Inigo Jones are far more often concerned with such affairs than with the provision of architectural designs.

Nevertheless, a steady flow of architectural designing was one of Jones's obligations. From the declared accounts we can list the successive projects for which designs were required and, in a rather limited number of cases, we have the relevant drawings by him. In his first year of office, 1615-16, Jones put in hand a number of smallish buildings at Newmarket, a place which James I had bought for the hunting and where he had already built himself a house. A brew-house and stable were the chief items, the stable [7, p. 33] being designed (though probably not executed) in a romantic style close to some of the masque drawings. At the same time, the Queen commissioned Inigo to build a new house for her at her palace of Greenwich, the house known ever since as the Queen's House. In 1617-18 he built an ornamental gateway for her at Oatlands and in the same year came a new buttery at St James's for Prince Charles. To 1617 probably belongs a design, never executed, for a new Star Chamber. In 1619-20 a new lodging – in fact, a large house – was built for the King's favourite, the Marquis (Duke from 1623) of Buckingham, at Whitehall; while at Newmarket another great 'lodging' was built for the occasional residence of Prince Charles. In January 1619 the Banqueting House at Whitehall was burnt down; a new one of much greater height and pretensions was begun, and finished in 1622. In 1623 the House of Lords was remodelled with a new roof and ceiling, a new stable was begun at

Theobalds and orders were given for a new chapel at St James's for the use of the Spanish princess whom Prince Charles went to Spain to marry but whom he returned without. At the same time the chapel at Greenwich was remodelled and a park gateway built. In 1624 an open staircase into St James's Park was built at Whitehall and in 1625 a small Banqueting House (on the scale of a summer house) at Theobalds. That was the year of James I's death and Jones designed the catafalque for his funeral.

Such were the Surveyor's principal undertakings for James. Outside his official capacity he probably designed London houses for Sir Fulke Greville (Lord Brooke) in Holborn and Sir Edward Cecil in the Strand, a gateway and other things for Lord Arundel at Arundel House, a gateway (1621) at Chelsea for Lionel Cranfield and another for the Duke of Lennox at Ely Place, besides alterations (1622) at New Hall, Essex, for the Duke of Buckingham.

Here is ten years' work – in all, about sixteen items for the King and Queen and five or more for private persons of very high standing at court. Of all these things only four now survive – the Queen's House at Greenwich, the Banqueting House at Whitehall, the gateway for Chelsea (moved by Lord Burlington to Chiswick) and the Queen's Chapel at St James's. Of most of the remainder we have either sketches or records of very variable reliability. Of the St James's Buttery, Buckingham's lodging, the works at Theobalds and the Greenwich chapel we know no more than what we can gather from the declared accounts – and that is little. Taking all the evidence together, what can we make of it? Remembering the immaturity of Jones's designs before 1615, how far does the work of the next decade show a consistent and mature approach? What sort of an architect was Inigo Jones between the ages of forty-two and fifty-two?

Ten Years' Work: 1615-25

Of Jones's attitude to architecture in the year that he became Surveyor we have invaluable evidence in a note he wrote in his Roman sketchbook. He says that in his opinion the 'composed ornaments' brought in by Michelangelo and his followers are inappropriate to what he calls 'sollid Architecture' and the façades of houses, and should be reserved for garden architecture and interiors. In the expression 'composed ornaments' he doubtless includes the intricately profiled cornices and architraves, broken pediments, swagged tablets and enriched panels exhibited by most of the modern buildings in the Rome he saw in 1614 – in short, the paraphernalia of what we call Mannerism. He is not contemptuous of these things which can, on proper occasion, be exciting and admirable but he believes they are secondary to fundamentally disciplined architecture – 'sollid, proporsionable according to the rulles, masculine and unaffected.'

This would be the almost inevitable view of an intelligent English critic of 1615, for two reasons. First, because of the nauseating proliferation of Mannerist ornament – 'the monstrous Babels of our Moderne Barbarisme' as Chapman called it – in English 'Jacobean' building. Second, because of the tremendous pull of the authentic antique, as presented by Vitruvius and the Italian theorists, in any mind sufficiently travelled and educated to understand what it was all about. Anybody who had seen the antique in Rome, who had been attracted to Palladio and talked with Scamozzi, would tend to take the 'masculine and unaffected' view. It was not a view which prevailed in Italy but it was built in to Italian theory and to foreign eyes it might very well seem, as it obviously did to Jones, that contemporary Italian architecture was tired and going badly off the rails. The important thing was to become seized of the rails.

It was Italian theory to which Jones attached himself and all his buildings attest his scrupulous reading and observation of its chief exponents. Up to

1615, his main sources were obviously Vitruvius (Barbaro's edition), Serlio and Palladio. Scamozzi's *Idea* was only published in 1615. It was in Jones's hands by 25 March 1617, the date inscribed in his own copy, and is at once reflected in a sketch for the Newmarket brew-house dating from that year. Jones, in his notes, is sometimes very critical of Scamozzi and considers that he distorted or misunderstood Palladio. Scamozzi's illustrations, on the other hand, he thoroughly digested and they are reflected over and over again in his work.

All three of these authors – Serlio, Palladio and Scamozzi – are reflected in the designs of 1615-25. Serlio, of course, is the least disciplinary of the three: his books are encyclopedic, presenting a mass of material rather coarsely, the later books being very miscellaneous treasuries of designs. Jones went to Serlio not for discipline but for ideas; and having seized an idea he altered and refined it in the light of the geometrical procedure implicit in Alberti, Palladio and Scamozzi. Beautiful examples of this are the designs for gateways for Oatlands (1617) and Arundel House (1618) [27, p. 66]. Isolated courtyard gateways had long been popular in England: the well-known examples (of Serlian derivation) at Holdenby, Northamptonshire, are dated 1583. But Jones brings a fresh intelligence to the type. Behind both these designs is a Serlio original but every single element in it has been altered to fall into a new modular harmony. The Mannerist romantic nonsense is brought within the range of 'sollid Architecture'.

But these, though significant, are trifles. The Queen's House at Greenwich, begun in 1616, presented a weightier challenge. It was to be a house in two parts – one within the Palace precincts and the other in Greenwich Park, the two parts being connected by a covered bridge crossing a public road [9]. Lorenzo de Medici's villa at Poggio a Caiano (finished by Giuliano da Sangallo in 1485) has a similar plan-shape, though the connecting link is a great hall, not a bridge. The Medici villa also has an open colonnade like that built into the park front at Greenwich [8]; the

8. Greenwich. The Queen's House, south front, finished 1635

9. Greenwich. The Queen's House, begun 1616

10. Greenwich. The Queen's House, north front, finished 1635

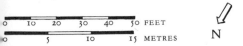

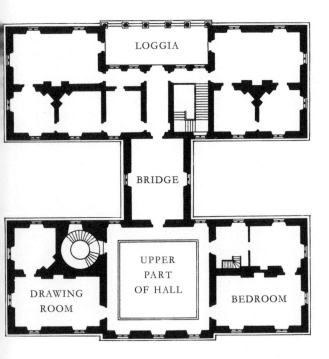

LOGGIA

BRIDGE

UPPER
PART
OF HALL

DRAWING
ROOM

BEDROOM

wide spaced windows at Greenwich, the terrace on the palace side [10] and even the curved steps leading to it all derive from Poggio a Caiano. The detailed working out, both in plan and elevation, is more severe than Giuliano's, however, and rests on Jones's studies of Palladio and Scamozzi. The forty-foot cubic hall is the first of those monumental interiors based on cubes or multiples or subdivisions of cubes which must have seemed to Jones, all through his career, to have the ineffable nobility of the absolute.

Work at the Queen's House stopped when Anne died in 1619, and was only resumed, for Henrietta Maria, in 1630 and completed in 1635. We cannot be absolutely sure that it was finished as first designed, but the essence

of it must belong to 1616. Today (as the Maritime Museum) it is much impoverished by the bareness of its interiors and, externally, by the fact that the division between the two separate parts was closed up (in 1661) to obtain more accommodation. But it is still, if one thinks about it, an extraordinary performance – this *quattrocento* idea of a Roman patrician villa, brought to the Thames, subjected to the full rigour of Palladio and Scamozzi, and resolved into such a serene and simple statement that it might as easily belong to 1816 as 1616. Jones as a prophet of neo-Classicism is a subject we shall enter upon later. Here is a first hint.

In June 1617 it was reported that Inigo Jones had made a design for a new Star Chamber and that the King would build it if money could be found. It would be in character for James I to fancy the idea of a splendid new setting for the modern Solomon in his own paramount court of jurisdiction. But the designs – still existing – remained on paper. Then, on 12 January 1619, the Banqueting House in Whitehall was destroyed by fire. As to the rebuilding of this there could be no question. Money was at once found, a design and estimate were produced by 19 April. A special commission was appointed and the building accounts opened on 1 June. They closed on 31 March 1622, with the building complete.

The design for the Star Chamber [11 and 12] and the designs for the new Banqueting House [13 and 14] must be considered together. We ought perhaps at the same time to recall the old Banqueting House with whose interior, at least, Jones was probably associated. Here, then, are three classical chambers, designed respectively in 1606, 1617 and 1619. All we can say of the first is that it was, roughly speaking, on the basilica model, with galleries, aisles, and two orders of columns. The Star Chamber design has, similarly, two orders but, there being no galleries or aisles, they are backed against the walls as half-columns; and at one end is a columned niche with its own smaller order. The Roman basilica idea is thus neatly expressed without being fully articulated in a project which,

11. Design for Star Chamber, 1617 (re-drawn by Webb)

12. Plan for Star Chamber, 1617

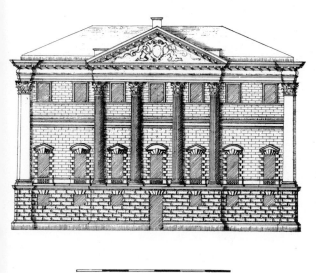

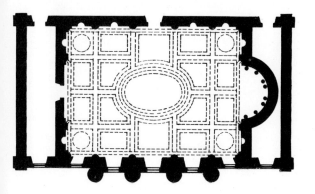

being for the administration of justice, has a special affinity with the basilica idea. Then comes the new Banqueting House. Here the same theme is taken and greatly enlarged. The Star Chamber was to be seventy-six feet long. The interior of the Banqueting House is half as long again.

The Banqueting House was conceived as the nave of a basilica on a grand scale. If, today, this is not at once apparent it is because the great

13. Whitehall. The Banqueting House, 1619–22, plan

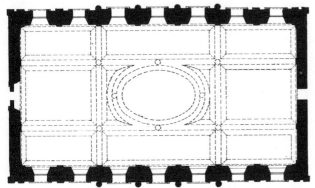

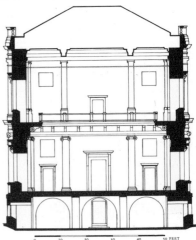

14. Whitehall. The Banqueting House, 1619–22

ehall. The Banqueting House (after the restoration of 1965)

16. Whitehall. The Banqueting House.
Design for the great door, 1619

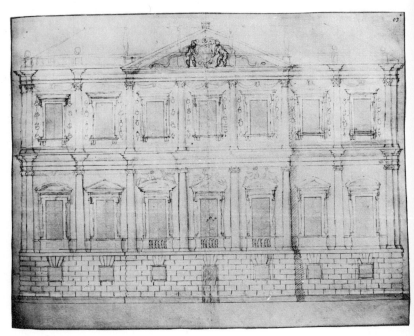

17. Whitehall. Design for the Banqueting House, 1619

niche, or apse, is missing. As completed in 1622, this feature occupied the south end to about half its height and at once gave the interior a sense of direction – almost like a church. Its upper part was a semi-dome and the accounts mention 'the ribbes of the fretworke of the great Neech' which probably means that this semi-dome was coffered like the apses in the temple of Venus and Rome as restored by Palladio. The 'neech' was abolished very early – probably in 1625-6 – and the Banqueting House is the poorer. A vast double cube, held in space by two splendid orders – Ionic and Corinthian – under and over a cantilevered gallery, and covered by a beamed ceiling in whose panels Rubens's apotheosis of James I was fixed in 1635, the interior has a formidable and even forbidding immobility [15].

18. Whitehall. The Banqueting House (in 1965)

Jones's thoughts on the basilica as a theme, deriving from Palladio's researches, are in fact an integration of cognate themes expressed not only in Palladio's restored Roman basilica, but in his version of the Egyptian Hall and some temple reconstructions. These prototypes provided ample material for the interior and could be set off by elements reflecting contemporary Mannerism, as we see in the fine drawing for a door-case [16]. But for the exteriors they provided nothing whatever. Thus, for the exterior of the Star Chamber he looked to Scamozzi and adopted the main features of the elevation of a large villa, raising it on a rusticated basement. Similarly for the Banqueting House he went to Palladio and borrowed part of the elevation of a study for a town house, again raising it on a basement and omitting (after some hesitation) the central pediment with which it was crowned. These borrowings are not important as such; they are simply choices of diagrammatic arrangement. The Star Chamber elevation, however, really is something of a pastiche, and a bad one, with the windows peculiar to Palladio's Palazzo Thiene crammed into a framework drawn from Scamozzi and totally alien to them in character.

The Banqueting House façade [18 and 19] is a different matter altogether, and a wonderfully harmonious design. The Palladian diagram borrowed for the exterior coincides nicely with the scheme of the interior, which is to say that it prescribes seven bays of superimposed columns; as in the interior, Jones made the lower order Ionic and the upper an improvisation on the Composite. The diagram also prescribed a division in the façade giving prominence to the three middle bays. The interest of the work, however, lies less in the diagram than in its detailed development. Perhaps the first thing to observe and remember about the Banqueting House is that the normal wall surface is rusticated almost from top to bottom, all horizontal and vertical joints being firmly cut into a V. The effect of this is that there is no 'dead' surface larger than a single stone and that anything superposed on the pattern of rustication must justify itself either by strength of relief or intensity of contrast. Jones uses both. At each end of the façade is a pair of coupled pilasters, their two nearly-joined areas of plain surface effectively quelling the force of the rustication as it approaches the corners. Next inwards comes a single pilaster between two windows (deliberately the weakest area), then a column in the round which, however, is not quite in the round because beyond it the wall surface presses forward to claim half its thickness. The next column is a half-column on this advanced surface and this brings us to the centre. This subtle increase both in advance and relief in the middle three bays gives the façade its fullness and vitality. Much of the art, however, is in the orders of columns themselves. The columns are unfluted and nakedly smooth against the rigorous crust of rusticated wall, a sensuous combination reminiscent of Giulio Romano from whom, indeed, it probably comes through the Palazzo Thiene – the one building by Palladio where Giulio's influence is paramount. The friezes of the orders are unenriched but, ranging with the capitals of the upper order, is a sub-frieze of masks and swags. This, the only piece of naturalistic carving in the building, rhythmically celebrates the ascendancy of the orders over the mechanic harshness of V-jointed stones.

The façade of the Banqueting House towards Whitehall is, of course, the most conspicuous and famous of all Inigo Jones's works. Which being so, it must be said at once that not a stone of it belongs to the seventeenth century. It was originally in three stones – brown Oxfordshire for the basement, a dun-coloured Northamptonshire for the upper walls and white Portland only for the orders and balustrade. This quiet polychromy was eliminated when Sir John Soane refaced nearly the whole front (and the duplicate in the court behind) with Portland in 1829. Soane, however, reproduced the original details with scrupulous care and the façade may even have gained a little from two centuries of practice in the cutting of classical ornaments. The present sash windows are another change; Jones's windows were of the mullion-and-transom type.

One would not suppose, looking at the Banqueting House, that it was designed for the presentation of masques, and in fact there is no reason to suppose that the architect kept that consideration uppermost. Whenever a masque *was* presented, the interior of the building was transformed, with the lower windows wholly obliterated by banks of seats. That, however, was only once or twice a year. For most of the time it was used for formal receptions by the King and in the basement was a place with a 'rock' and 'shell worke' and presumably a fountain, used for drinking parties.

As first built, in the setting of the Tudor Palace of Whitehall, the Banqueting House was something altogether anomalous. An English critic of 1621 found it 'too faire and nothing suitable to the rest of the house'. An Italian of the period would have found it disconcerting – obviously, a *palazzo* on the grandest scale but of very small extent. He would have been astonished to learn that it contained nothing but one huge *sala* and would have demanded to know when and on what lines the rest of the palace was to proceed. We may well ask the same. Unhappily there is no answer. That James I and his architect considered the building a fragment of a greater whole is sufficiently proved by the fact that, as completed, it not only had no proper end elevations but no staircase except a makeshift affair jutting out on the north. But it is not until 1638 that we hear of proposals for a comprehensive rebuilding of Whitehall. That was an ambition of Charles I. If the seeds of it were already in his father's mind in 1619, no document exists to confirm the fact.

There was, of course, very little money in James's exchequer and, furthermore, he had building commitments of importance elsewhere. In the same year that the Banqueting House was begun he was building, next to the Privy Garden at Whitehall, a house for his Master of the Horse, the

20. Design for the Prince's Lodging, Newmarket, probably as executed, 1619

21. Design, probably for the Prince's Lodging, Newmarket, 1619

Marquis of Buckingham. Of this only one record survives – a coloured drawing by Jones, probably of the dining-room ceiling [25]. It is in timber, coffered and richly moulded, based on Palladio's illustration of the cella ceiling in a building which he identifies as the Temple of Neptune.

James I was also building again at Newmarket. This time it was a 'lodging' for Prince Charles and, although records of the completed structure are entirely lacking, there fortunately survive two façade designs, one of which [20] almost certainly represents what was built. The other [21] has many of the same features and although it may conceivably be for another house altogether it is obviously of similar date with the first and a comparison of the two designs is extremely interesting. The second design is a façade of the type of Palladio's town-house for the Capra family in Vicenza, but expanded with reference to a Scamozzi design and containing some Serlian detail, notably the rusticated round-headed entry. It is apparently assembled on a module which is the width of all windows except the centre window. The middle section is a square of eight modules, and the façade is divided horizontally in the ratio of three to five by the string-course over the lower windows. The whole width of the front is approximately seventeen modules which, if we give a value of four feet to the module suggests a total width of sixty-eight feet.

The first design appears to be for a house of the same width, dimensions on the drawing approximating to a total of sixty-eight feet. Nearly all the same features are present, the notable exceptions being the columns. The ratios are quite different and in determining them Jones has taken into account a high roof with large pedimented dormer windows. The ground floor is reduced to a mere basement with an eight-foot ceiling and the whole design is more tightly knit than the first. It is also much more interesting and expressive. The decisive contrast between the verticality of the pedimented centre and the strong horizontality of the whole partly accounts for this, and this design is more acutely felt as a cohesive pattern, cohesion being agreeably stressed by the continuous string-course at the level of the window-heads. The cornice arrangement, too, is interesting. The middle section has a regular entablature under the pediment and the cornice of this goes all round the building. But the frieze and architrave change abruptly when they leave the centre and become, in effect, the two overlapping planes of a very big architrave, this big architrave with the cornice directly above making an effective transition to the heavy and conspicuous roof.

Altogether, this design for the Prince's Lodging represents a great advance in Jones's maturity as a classical designer. He can lay aside diagrams borrowed from Palladio and Scamozzi; he can be classical while dispensing altogether with columns. He is his own master.

Of the plan of the Prince's Lodging at Newmarket we have no drawing, but we do know that the building extended back forty-four feet, and it happens that, allowing for centre projections back and front and customary wall-thicknesses, this dimension provides for an apartment twenty feet wide and forty feet deep in the middle of the house. The height of this apartment could not have been much more or less than twenty feet, the three dimensions together constituting a double cube. Almost certainly, therefore, a double-cube hall extended through the house on the first floor. The Presence and Privy Chambers were, doubtless, on one side, the Bed Chamber and Withdrawing Chamber on the other. As in the Queen's House, there was a winding stair. If we look ahead for a moment to Wilton, we shall notice how close the ratios of the main front are to those of the Prince's Lodging. At Wilton, too, Jones made a double-cube room. It lies along the middle of the front instead of at right angles to it and measures thirty feet by sixty feet. At Wilton everything is on a larger scale. But the main decisions taken in designing the Prince's Lodging in 1619 account for nearly everything in the Wilton design of thirteen years later.

Closer in time to the Newmarket building is the still existing Queen's Chapel at St James's Palace and the connexion between these two is no less striking [22 and 23]. The Prince's Lodging was finished in 1621. In April 1623 Inigo Jones was ordered to design a new Chapel at St James's Palace for the reception of the Spanish Infanta, whom Prince Charles had gone to Spain to fetch as his bride. The foundation stone was laid on 16 May and the building prosecuted with great urgency until the news arrived that the Prince was returning without the Infanta. The building then proceeded at a more leisurely pace, but was ready for another Catholic bride, Henrietta Maria, whom Charles married shortly after his accession, in May 1625.

The Queen's Chapel at St James's consists mainly of a double-cube hall covered by a magnificent coffered ceiling of elliptical section. Westward of this is the Queen's Closet, a deep gallery originally separated from the chapel by a screen with Corinthian pilasters and festoons. The west front of the building is thus the front of this closet and the vestibule below it. Pressed to produce a design as quickly as possible, Jones has taken, so to speak, the 'middle slice' of the Prince's Lodging at Newmarket, rendering the double-cube hall as the chapel proper and reproducing the elements of the Newmarket elevation in that of the Queen's Closet. The resultant façade is, nevertheless, something totally different from the Newmarket centrepiece. The ratios are different, and the chapel is crowned not by an entablature but by a heavy 'block cornice' – a type of cornice with which the Romans were accustomed to finish massive stretches of plain walling. At once, a monumental note is sounded; the building is seen to be not a house but a temple. The interior of the chapel [26] is a double-cube of greater eloquence than the Banqueting House, partly, no doubt, because of the welcome curvature of the ceiling, but also because of the more interesting lighting. It is lit at the east end from a three-light window of the kind which the eighteenth century called 'Venetian' but which is rarely seen in Venice (Jones took it from Scamozzi who had used it conspicuously

James's Palace. The Queen's Chapel, 1623–7

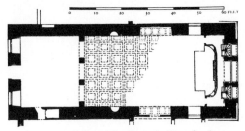

24. St James's Palace. The Queen's Chapel, 1623–7

in the street front of his Palazzo Trissino in Vicenza). Carved angels fly with an armorial cartouche above the arch while garlands fall across it to the lower lights.

The ceiling is as close to the archaeologizing spirit of Neo-classicism as anything in Jones's work at this period. Though constructed of timber, it is modelled on the coffered masonry barrel-vault of the temple of Venus and Rome as restored by Palladio. As a classical study it may be compared with the ceiling design for the Marquis of Buckingham's dining room, already mentioned [25]. An even more interesting comparison might be with a structure by Jones of which, however, we know so little that it can only be mentioned in passing – the reconstructed House of Lords of 1623-4. On the ancient walls of this building Jones raised a new covering in the form of a plaster barrel-vault. This was painted by the Serjeant Painter 'with curious stonework in distemper'. Hollar's portrayal of the trial of Archbishop Laud in 1644 shows the vault and the painting, which seems to have

25. Design, probably for the Marquis of Buckingham's lodging, Whitehall, 1619

26. St James's Palace. The Queen's Chapel, 1623–7, interior

imitated square coffers. We cannot be sure, but it seems possible that here Jones, with the painter's help, was attempting a *trompe l'œil* representation of the model he so much admired in Palladio — the model which, almost at the same time, he was copying in beautifully executed timber at St James's – though there on a smaller scale and with a more modest curvature.

Of other buildings undertaken by Jones before the death of James I there is, unfortunately, not one of any size which can be described with confidence. There are indeed, the decorative archways designed for Lord Arundel [27], Lionel Cranfield [28] and the Duke of Lennox [29]. Of these, only the second exists, having been moved from Chelsea to Lord Burlington's Chiswick villa where it still stands. Sensitive and exact

7. (*Opposite*) Gateway at Arundel House, 1619

8. Gateway from the Great House, Chelsea, 1621, now in Chiswick Park

essays in Italian Mannerism, these things are perhaps less remarkable in themselves than because they are from an English hand. A curious structure called the Park Stairs – a covered stairway descending into St James's Park from the first floor of a house connecting with Whitehall Palace – is shown in two or three paintings. Part of it is in the nature of a double verandah with balustrades, columns and a scrolled pediment, but the illustrations hardly permit us to see it as Jonesian architecture.

The last structure by Jones associated with James I was the 'hearse' or catafalque for his enormously expensive funeral. The fine drawing for it survives at Oxford [30]. The idea behind it is Bramante's *tempietto*, but it is reduced to an octagon, and the columns are pressed back against their respondent pilasters to make piers which not only carry the attic storey and dome but provide positions for seated mourning figures. This ingenious and logical contraction of a famous model rises from a platform with standing figures at the corners. The figures were carved by Le Sueur and the whole thing was painted by De Critz, the Serjeant Painter. The structure, thirty-five feet high, must have stood in Westminster Abbey, where James I was buried on 7 May 1625.

Philosophy: Architecture

In his copy of an Italian translation of Plutarch's *Moralia,* probably acquired in Venice in 1614, Inigo Jones marks with special approval a passage in which the author draws an analogy between music and medicine. The composer, says Plutarch, does not achieve perfection by doing away with sharpness and flatness, nor does the physician achieve health in a body by eliminating heat or cold. The extremes are to be reduced to that moderation within which harmony and health are to be found. This Platonic view of affairs Jones held with conviction and it is clearly reflected in his architecture. There is 'hot' and there is 'cold', but never are the two brought into conflict. There is warm invention, but no design is ever scorched by it. There is sheer, cold identification with the antique, but never so much as would mark Jones as a copyist. In terms of the generalizing discriminations of modern scholarship one could say that Jones is sometimes 'Mannerist' and sometimes 'neo-Classicist', that his performance is in suspension between the two and his felicity in their interplay. If this is true and he is able to bring the two attitudes into one, his own, it is because of a third tension – a philosophical rather than a formal one. At the core of his architectural thinking is the belief that design is an affair of number, of procedure by natural subdivision. To this absolute control all invention and all imitation are subordinate. The ancient orders were and are to be controlled by the module. Larger elements in building are to be thought out on the basis of squares and cubes and their simplest rational sub-divisions. Hence the cubic hall at Greenwich, the double cubes at Whitehall, Newmarket and the St James's chapel.

Hence also Jones's curious elucidation of the problem of Stonehenge when challenged by James I, staying, on progress, with the Earl of Pembroke at Wilton in 1620. Stonehenge, he declared, was Roman. Having surveyed the monument and plotted its plan he had found it to be based on

four intersecting equilateral triangles. This was precisely the diagram which Palladio had deduced, from Vitruvius' account, to be the basis of the ancient type of theatre. Therefore, Stonehenge, notwithstanding the barbaric crudity of its masonry, issued from a Roman mind. If, to us, the solution is ludicrous, we must also admit it to have been, in its time, intelligent. It was developed and published as a book by John Webb in 1655 with a large and tedious overlay of his own scholarship.

Behind Jones the architect there is always Jones the philosopher, a shining intelligence in the lay intellectual circles which became a power in English society under James I. How, in these circles, he was admired and looked up to is attested by occasional dedications and references. Edmund Bolton's aspirations for Jones have been quoted. When Bolton proposed to the King in 1617 an academy of scholars to be affiliated to the Order of the Garter, Jones was listed in the corporation of 'essentials'. George Chapman, dedicating his miniature *Musaeus* to Jones in 1616, recognized a fellowship between his own art and Jones's; 'Ancient Poesie, and ancient Architecture, requiring to their excellence a like creating and proportionable Rapture'. Ben Jonson, until his differences with Jones burst into a furious quarrel, had an unlimited admiration for the King's Surveyor, 'full of noble observation of Antiquitie, and high Presentment'.

The last quotation is from a printed text of the *Masque of Augurs*, the first masque to be presented in the great new Banqueting House just completed in 1622. There survives only one rough sketch of the scene – a street lined with monumental buildings, terminating in something like the Pantheon. Of the scenes for later masques up to 1625 we have little knowledge, but there is one extremely interesting sketch which cannot be attached to any of the masques but which almost certainly dates from this period. It is inscribed 'Cupids Pallas' and shows, as does the *Augurs* sketch, a classical building standing at the end of a classical street [31]. Of the buildings on either side (actually, the same building drawn to different scales) only the corners are shown; they are palaces with a giant Corinthian order standing on a rusticated basement and rising through two storeys, reminding one of the elevations for the proposed Star Chamber. The building which closes the vista, though not fully worked out, is very remarkable. It is on a square plan and the façade is of equal breadth and height up to the main entablature which, with a parapet, stands outside and over the square. There are two orders – Ionic below and Corinthian above – in almost exactly the ratio of those at the Banqueting House; and as in that building, the ends of the composition are closed by coupled pilasters. The lower storey is entirely open. The fenestration of the upper storey is that of the St James's chapel – and thus, of course, approximately that of the Prince's Lodging at Newmarket. Through the unglazed windows can just be seen a flat coffered ceiling such as Jones may have designed for Buckingham's lodging.

The design summarizes, faithfully and felicitously, Jones's architectural preferences as we find them in the chief buildings of the first decade of his Surveyorship. Its Italian relationships are obvious: one can even see the central building as an extremely delicate variation on Sansovino's Libreria Vecchia. It is this feeling for variation, for combining familiar elements in a fresh way, together with the classical reserve and the strong sense of a transparent geometry which makes it unequivocally a work of Jones.

The Royal Works of Charles I

Inigo Jones was actively in charge of King Charles's Works from his accession in 1625 till the disruption caused by the outbreak of civil war in 1642 – a period of seventeen years. The immediately striking thing about the list of undertakings which can be extracted from the declared accounts for this period is that the most interesting and costly of them were all for the Queen – Henrietta Maria. For her were the improvements at Somerset House – the Cabinet Room, the new River Stairs, the fountains and cistern-house, the refitting of the Cross Gallery and, most important of all, the new chapel. For her the Queen's House at Greenwich, a neglected carcase since Anne of Denmark's death, was completed and equipped. For her the 'pergola' to the Withdrawing Chamber at St James's was built. And for her, too, were the arbour and the redecorated lodging with its new balcony at Oatlands.

Of the work at Somerset House, her London palace, almost the only records we have concern the River Stairs and the chapel. The stairs (1628-32) can be seen in Kip's view of *c.* 1700 and again, in sharp perspective, in Canaletto's view of London from the terrace; but unfortunately we cannot rely on either. Though both show the elegant gate-piers crowned by vases, they differ in all else and Kip, the earlier of the two, shows two relief carvings of river gods mounted on the balustrade, which can hardly have been their original position. By Canaletto's time they had gone and scrolls were substituted. Successive reconstructions must have spoiled this design, in which Jones surely had in mind the stair leading to Michelangelo's Palazzo Senatorio which has river gods in the spandrils of the stair.

We are scarcely more fortunate with the chapel. Its plan we know and in Kip we can see the cruciform lead roof. There are three alternative designs

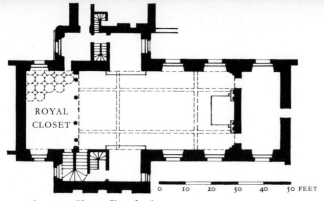

32. Somerset House Chapel, 1630–5

by Jones for a niche and one for a window; and there are good eighteenth-century engravings of the ceiling and the screen to the Royal Closet [33]. These do not add up to a representation of the chapel, but with their aid and, in addition, some dimensions extracted from the accounts, we can place it without much difficulty in the perspective of Jones's development.

The Somerset House chapel may have been designed as early as 1623 when chapels both there and at St James's were ordered, but it was only begun in 1630 and finished five years later; important details are dated 1632. It was certainly rather like the St James's chapel, but a trifle larger, the body of the building being a double cube sixty feet long. At the north (liturgical 'west') was the Royal Closet, at the south ('east') a vestry-house and the whole building was somewhat shut in. The ceiling, instead of being elliptical and coffered as at St James's was flat and beamed – a variant on the Banqueting House. A rather special feature was the screen to the closet [33] with a fluted Doric order below, in stone, and terms with a decorative cresting, in timber, above. The very open Doric spacing, with column and pier at either end, may be compared with the Ionic spacing in 'Cupids Pallas'. Looking ahead, we may also see the design reflected in the pier-and-column closures of the portico at St Paul's. The Doric entablature is remarkable for the substitution of scrolls for triglyphs,

33. Somerset House Chapel. Screen to the Queen's Closet, *c*.1632

77

an idea which Jones took (as we learn from a note in his Vitruvius) from an antique marble at Arundel House. But if the Doric is treated in the true research spirit of neo-Classicism, the superstructure is a delicate piece of Mannerist ornamentalism. Mannerism we find again in the window design [34] – a soberly composed derivative of Michelangelo, perhaps through Fontana. Altogether, the interweaving of neo-Classical and Mannerist thought seems to have been as marked in the Somerset House chapel as we have found it elsewhere; but of the total effect of the building we are, and are likely to remain, in ignorance.

Baffled as we are by so much at Somerset House, it is perhaps worth trying to conjure up from the accounts some idea of the richly decorated new Cabinet Room, created by Jones and the painter, Matthew Goodrich,

34. Somerset House Chapel. Design for a window, 1632

in 1628-30 in a small building some twenty years older, westward of the Cross Gallery. It was completely panelled, each panel having 'grotesques' on a white ground, while the stiles and muntins were enriched with gilded and shadowed guilloche with small flowers at the crossings. The ceiling was white with a central circular panel marked with a leaf-enriched moulding, shadowed and gilded. The entablature, too, had shadowed and gilded mouldings. A stone window had gold arabesques on its white surfaces and an edge of gold next to the glass; hinges, lock and staples were gilded. The chimney-piece had an Ionic order below painted like white marble, gilded, and above, a Corinthian order in blue and gold. The door-case was painted like white marble, with enrichments picked out in gold. Outside the window which looked over the river, the balcony rails were painted cobalt blue, with the stanchions, iron balls and other details gilded, the four consoles supporting it in blue and gold. Marble-white, blue and gold, with nearly every surface decorated: the effect would be somewhat that of so many of the richly painted tombs of the period, but cooler and more classical. Nothing quite of this kind now exists in England.

Works at Somerset House, of one sort or another, continued through the whole of Charles I's reign, and in 1638 there was evidently a monumental scheme for rebuilding along the Strand. The elevation of this is, as we shall see, closely related to an even greater palace project – that for Whitehall where, meanwhile, there was little to show except the remodelling as a theatre of the interior of Henry VIII's octagonal Cockpit [35]. Half this octagon was adapted as a small auditorium of the same shape; the other half was filled by a stage, a classical 'scene' on a segmental curve, and the space behind it. John Webb's rather coarse drawing of the scene does not make it seem attractive, but we must think of it alongside the exquisite Somerset House screen. As a study in attached orders we can compare it with the early design for St Paul's west front and the later design for the screen at Winchester.

35. Whitehall Palace. The Cockpit Theatre, 1629 (re-drawn by Webb)

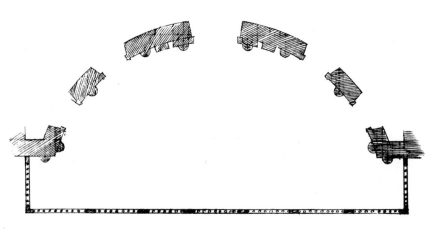

At St James's Jones designed, besides the 'pergola' already mentioned (a double flight of steps leading down from a terrace to the garden), a modest sculpture gallery in the orchard, to contain the antique pieces which Charles I had bought from the Duke of Mantua. It consisted of a Doric or Tuscan colonnade of fifteen columns, with grilles in the openings, set parallel with the orchard wall. The beams connecting the columns to the wall were cantilevered out into St James's Park to provide a covered stretch of ground where the King could ride in bad weather – an ingenious extension of the design, which Webb instanced as an application of the principle of the Tuscan atrium. No doubt it was consciously that, for at the time it was built the Tuscan order was very much in Jones's thoughts. It was, indeed, to be the theme of one of the most remarkable of all his works – Covent Garden.

Covent Garden

Covent Garden – the square, the church and the adjoining streets – was the undertaking of a private individual and had nothing to do with the royal Works except in so far as the head of the Works, Inigo Jones, was *ex officio* involved in it. He was involved rather deeply and the circumstances were as follows.

The ground of Covent Garden belonged to Francis, fourth Earl of Bedford, a man of large business capacity and initiative, not a favourite at court and in fact tending to hold dangerously independent views. In face of proclamations prohibiting building in the neighbourhood of London, he had attempted to build for profit in Long Acre and been stopped. Any attempt to develop Covent Garden would have been stopped, but the Earl approached this major project with more circumspection. By what stages he attained his goal we do not know but in 1631 he obtained a licence to build as many 'houses and buildings fitt for the habitacons of *Gentlemen* and men of abillity' as he should think proper. There was no mention of any payment by the Earl but we know in fact that the licence cost him two thousand pounds.

How Inigo Jones, the King's Surveyor, came to be employed on the work is not obvious from the documents, but inferences can be drawn. The Proclamation of 2 May 1625 was in the nature of an absolute prohibition of any building whatever except on old foundations. The commissioners appointed to implement the Proclamation, however, were given some latitude. Nothing was said about building on old foundations and authority was given to any four commissioners, *of whom the King's Surveyor of Works was to be one,* to allot ground for the rebuilding of houses in such a way as to achieve 'Uniformitie and Decency'. This still did not allow for any increase in the number of houses but it did facilitate planned re-distribution and, more significantly, established the principle that any

36. Covent Garden (detail of the aerial view by W. Hollar, *c.* 1640)

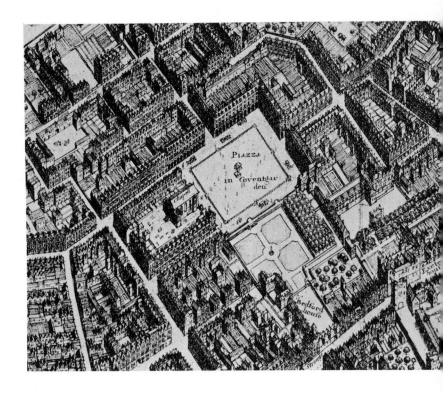

37. Covent Garden (etching by W. Hollar, c.1658)

new-shaping of London's streets should come under the eye of the King's
Surveyor – in other words, Inigo Jones. The text of the licence in no way
diminished the force of this and the employment of Jones was, in effect,
a condition imposed on the licensee.

In the licence there is no mention of a church, but we have clear evidence
elsewhere that the church got into the scheme because the Earl of Bedford
was shrewd enough to see that the scheme would not work without one.
It was a matter of expediency rather than piety; it rendered possible the
creation of a new quarter, ready provided with the proper symbol of social
acceptability. The idea of church and square as a calculated ensemble is
remarkable for this date, but its derivation is not in doubt. John Evelyn
picked up the information that it was the church and piazza at Leghorn
which 'gave the first hint to the building both of the church and Piazza in
Covent Garden'. This was certainly the case. Under Ferdinando Medici,
who succeeded to the Dukedom of Tuscany in 1587, Leghorn was rapidly
transformed from almost nothing to the great international sea-port which
it was to remain for two hundred years. The building of the cathedral and
the piazza were part of this planned development – at the time, possibly
the most ambitious town-planning project to be found anywhere. Jones

would have seen it on his first Italian visit and the Earl of Bedford would have heard of it. Now, Duke Ferdinando's niece was Marie de Medicis, Queen of Henri iv of France, and *his* initiative in creating the Place Royale in Paris in 1605 probably derived from Leghorn. The Place Royale, which Jones will have seen in progress in 1609, has a distinct bearing on Covent Garden. And the long arm of the Medicis stretches even further when we consider that Henrietta Maria, Charles i's queen, was Marie de Medicis' daughter. The dynastic network apart, however, links between London and Leghorn, direct or via Paris, are not far to seek. The architectural common factors in the three schemes are less important than the idea, common to all three, of rationalizing a residential quarter on architectural as well as profitable lines. In the first two cases the initiative was that of the sovereign; in the third, characteristically for England, that of a subject at loggerheads with his sovereign.

Church and houses were begun almost simultaneously, in 1631. The form to be taken by the church raised a curious question. No church had been built on a new site in London since the reformation. There had been rebuildings, like St Katharine Cree, on more or less traditional lines.

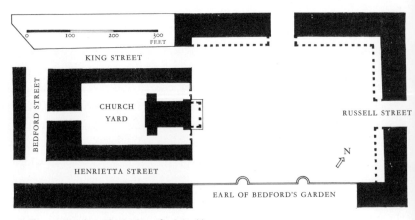

38. Covent Garden. Block plan of original lay-out

Jones himself, as we have seen, had built one chapel royal and was building another – both for Catholic worship, however. No new pattern had ever been proposed for an absolutely new Protestant church. What should its form be ? No echo has reached us of the debates which must have been held on this point. We have only the result on which to base our own speculations; and the result is, approximately, a temple. The Earl of Bedford, not a high churchman, would require simplicity; Jones would need to seek specific architectural terms. As it happens, the attitudes of both men are neatly enfolded in an anecdote – an anecdote pregnant with more meaning than is generally ascribed to it. It was told to Walpole by Mr Speaker Onslow and Walpole's version is as follows :

> When the Earl of Bedford sent for Inigo he told him he wanted a chapel for the parishioners of Covent Garden, but added he would not go to any considerable expense; 'In short', said he, 'I would not have it much better than a barn.' 'Well! then', said Jones, 'You shall have the handsomest barn in England.'

The manifest point of the story is the antithesis between the financier's dour economic challenge and the artist's gay paradoxical response; and that is good enough. But there may be a little more to it. The anecdote may have been in origin an anecdote about the Tuscan order.

Inigo Jones's feeling for the Tuscan order, manifesting itself at various stages of his career, is one of the most interesting aspects of his neo-Classicism. The Tuscan has always been recognized as the most primitive of the five orders – the closest to the vernacular. Vitruvius gives a very incomplete formula but makes it clear that it is suitable only for timber beams and must have an enormous, truly sheltering eaves-spread – one quarter the height of the columns. Alberti did not think the Tuscan worth mentioning. Serlio fitted it into his arbitrary gamut of five rising orders by making it the dunce – squat and coarse, recommended for military architecture, city gates, arsenals and prisons. Palladio did not see it so but, taking into account the timber beams and wide-spaced columns, thought it appropriate to country buildings where the passage of carts was to be considered. Where all the authorities agree is on its plain, robust character. A church which was to be of the simplest, cheapest kind could not inappropriately be a temple structure incorporating the Tuscan order. As such it would have classical dignity at the vernacular level: it would be the 'handsomest barn' of the anecdote.

Jones had concerned himself with the Tuscan fifteen years before Covent Garden was begun, right at the outset of his surveyorship. As we have seen, there had been, in 1615-16, a question of designing various service buildings for King James I's new house at Newmarket. These included a stable and a brew-house – obvious subjects for the application of the Tuscan. For the stable he made a design [7] without an order at all but with romantically grotesque rustication recalling some of his masque designs. For the brew-house he designed something more sophisticated, taking Palladio's Villa Badoer as the diagrammatic basis but substituting in its six-column portico an arrangement of two Tuscan columns *in antis* which he found in Scamozzi. This arrangement, with arch-pierced walls connecting the antae to the main body of the building (as, for instance, in Palladio's Villa Rotonda) is an almost exact forecast of the portico at Covent Garden; on a small scale, of course, because the Newmarket design was for a very small building – the portico twenty-three feet across as against sixty feet at Covent Garden. The Newmarket design was never carried out. A brew-house was, indeed, built there in 1616-17, but it was twice the size and no portico is mentioned in the accounts. The Tuscan design was laid aside to come into its own at Covent Garden fifteen years later.

The Tuscan image varies from author to author and their graphic expositions are equally free. Scamozzi's version is a very tidy one, a kind of sub-Doric, avoiding the primitive earthiness which resides in or can be read into Vitruvius' account. In this, Scamozzi was following Palladio, who in turn followed Serlio. But Palladio, while giving his own polite paraphrase, also provided something which he had already worked out with Daniele Barbaro in his edition of Vitruvius, something much more arresting – a reconstruction following Vitruvius' text to the letter, with the plain, unmoulded beam and the huge projecting cantilevers or mutules. It was this raw, primitive presentation of the Tuscan which, astonishingly, appealed to Jones; he envisaged it perhaps as the order closest to natural ideas of construction. One is reminded of his equally astonishing but, in its way, logical attitude to Stonehenge.

Palladio's and Barbaro's Vitruvian version of the Tuscan was expounded by them as a piece of theoretical archaeologizing rather than as a specimen for imitation. But it was as real architecture that it appealed to Jones. He seems to have introduced it first in the sculpture gallery at St James's, already mentioned. Then, at Covent Garden he constructed a full-scale realization – columns $7\frac{1}{2}$ diameters high, with mutules one quarter the height of the columns, columns widely spaced and connected by massive timber beams [39]. It is an extraordinary performance, this Covent Garden portico; an archaeological essay unique, as Milizia declared, in the architecture of Europe and at the same time prophetic: prophetic of the theory and practice of neo-Classicism as it was to be understood more than a hundred years later.

The portico is not the whole church. It is, in fact, not even the main approach but only a monumental shelter with one sham and (originally) two real doors at the east end of the church and under the same roof. The church proper is a simple rectangular cell [40], a double square with a ceiling-height two thirds the side of the square. It is lit by very large round-headed windows with moulded architraves but no impost mouldings – a type which belongs to the *quattrocento* and in particular to Michelozzo but which Jones seems to give us for the naked logic of the thing.

39. St Paul's Church, Covent Garden, 1631 : restored after fire, 1795

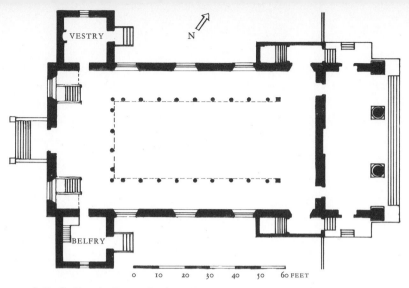

VESTRY

N

BELFRY

0   10   20   30   40   50   60 FEET

40. St Paul's Church, Covent Garden, 1631

41. St Paul's Church, Covent Garden, west front (view by P. Sandby, 1766)

The west end [41] is a copy of the east but without portico and therefore overwhelmingly severe. Vestries project on either side. Internally there were originally galleries and a perspective ceiling with a great painted cove by Matthew Goodrich. The church, all but the portico, stands in a church-yard. The approach to this – and thus to the great west door – was at first through two separately standing gateways on each side of the church, each consisting of an arch between pilasters, all rusticated, carrying an en-tablature and pediment [36]. These arches have disappeared but must be carefully considered in evaluating Jones's design. They were Tuscan, not of the order of the portico but based on a variant recorded both by Serlio and Palladio: the lower order of the Roman theatre at Verona. The con-nexion seems text-bookish but it does give rise to the speculation whether, in designing Covent Garden, Jones consciously adopted a Tuscan 'mood' for the whole. If we now turn from the church to the arcades and houses enclosing the space in front of it we may perhaps conclude that he did.

The two houses on the west side, to north and south of the church and separated from it by intervals in which stood the Verona-Tuscan gate-ways, are something of a mystery. Early views and the engraving in *Vitruvius Britannicus* show houses of obviously Jonesian proportions with pitched roofs containing dormers; but these must have disappeared before or soon after 1700, for all eighteenth-century views show entirely common-place houses on these sites. We have therefore no exact record of what Jones built and must pass at once to the ranges so well recorded by Sandby and Malton, on the north and east sides, the houses whose fronts stood on open arcades within which were the vaulted walks which, absurdly, be-came known as 'piazzas'. On the south side were no houses, only the wall of the Earl of Bedford's garden.

After the highly sophisticated use of sources in the design of the church, it is puzzling at first to find that the main source for the houses is one of Serlio's rather naive woodcuts. Yet it is natural enough. Jones uses Serlio here as he had used him for twenty years, as a source not for technique but for ideas. As long ago as 1608 he had based the design for the New Exchange in the Strand on a Serlian design for a similar type of building. Now he went to Serlio again for the sake of an idea expressed in a design for a great town house – '*Una habitatione per far dentro alla Citta in luogo nobile.*' Serlio's house has a steep roof with dormers '*alla Francese*' and, in its ground floor and mezzanine, the sort of arches which Jones was to build at Covent Garden, though in Serlio they are partly filled in and fitted as shops, '*fatta al costume di Roma*'. These arches Jones built not exactly as in the Serlio design but from a diagram in Book IV of the same author, in a section dealing with rustication and in fact demonstrating rustication as one of the attributes of the Tuscan. If we wish to regard Covent Garden as a continuous exercise in the Tuscan it seems that we may, nor does the design of the superstructure discourage the idea. Where Serlio put an Ionic order with pedestal, Jones merely uses plain pilaster strips running up to an eaves cornice equipped with brackets which belong to no particular order and are in fact a miniature variation of the mutules of the primitive Tuscan. Covent Garden therefore was Tuscan from beginning to end, a comprehensive essay in the Tuscan mood – Tuscan all the way from the high sophistication of the portico to the vernacular of the houses – a new vernacular, the first statement of what we naturally think of today as the Georgian house.

Jones's role as a forerunner of eighteenth-century neo-Classicism is impressively vested in the church and we can judge how strikingly his prophecy was fulfilled by the intense admiration awarded to it exactly a century after it was built. It was in 1734 that Ralph, the architectural critic, described Covent Garden church as 'without a rival, one of the most perfect pieces of architecture that the art of man can produce'; while to Thomas Malton, at the near end of the century, it was still 'one of the most perfect pieces of art ever produced in this country'. Such

42. Covent Garden. The 'piazzas', looking south-east (view by T. Sandby, 1768)

expressions may seem exaggerated but they are not difficult to understand in the light of eighteenth-century architectural thought. Covent Garden church would seem to Ralph to be architecture 'founded' – to quote Lord Shaftesbury – 'in truth and nature'; to Malton its bold simplicity would seem to justify the Abbé Laugier's enthronement of the primitive and his insistence on direct, uncomplicated expression.

Today, what exactly do we find at Covent Garden? As we pick our way among the bulging crates, the rackety trucks, the ancient vegetable stink, the presence of that portico is still tremendously felt. How much of it is original? It is certainly Jones's columns that we see and Jones's tough Tuscan version of a classical door-case inside. For the rest, it is mostly Georgian or Victorian reconstruction. In 1795 the church was gutted by fire. Restored externally with exact loyalty by Thomas Hardwick, the interior became a neat but uninteresting Georgian box. Hardwick substituted for Jones's stucco on the sides and west end a skin of Portland stone, but this was removed in a Victorian restoration and good red brick substituted. The Victorians also did away with the north and south walls of the portico, substituting arches. Worse than that, the ground-level of the market has at some time been raised, obscuring the plinth and steps on which the church stood. We miss the Verona-Tuscan gateways on either flank and, to enter the church today, we must walk round into Bedford Street or go through a hole in the wall in Henrietta Street. As for the houses and the 'piazzas', all are gone: the last of them went in the early thirties and nobody raised a hand in protest. On the north side, however, is a block called Bedford Chambers, built by the Duke of Bedford in 1880 to the design of his architect, Clutton. The lower storey is a competent, though not exact, imitation of the original piazzas. The upper part of the building is no more than a paraphrase of Jones, though a good one.

Although Jones certainly gave the designs for Covent Garden, his participation in its execution was probably slight; for the houses, anyway, it seems that Isaac de Caus was the executant architect. Jones was the King's Surveyor and fully occupied in the King's business which meant, as we have seen, a great deal more than making designs for buildings. It was, to be sure, as a royal official that he had been drawn into Covent Garden in the first place. His next great task was, similarly, one which had no direct connexion with the King's Works but in which royal prestige and authority were heavily involved. This was the restoration of St Paul's Cathedral.

St Paul's Cathedral

We have seen that among Jones's earliest architectural designs was one for a new termination to the Cathedral's central tower and another for a new west front. Both were decidedly immature and it was perhaps as well for Jones's credit that nothing whatever came of the King's gesture of 1608. In 1620, James I inaugurated another scheme. By this time Jones was his Surveyor of Works and was made a member of the Royal Commission which was to administer it. Quantities of Portland stone were brought to the site but subscriptions fell far short and the work stopped. Then, under Charles I, came Laud. William Laud was Bishop only from 1628 till 1633 when he went to Canterbury, but in those five years he procured finance sufficient to put in hand the first stage of a comprehensive restoration of the cathedral, a restoration so vigorous that, seen from some points of view, it was to appear virtually a new building. In 1631, a new commission was set up, this time without Jones, who was made honorary architect, with a paid deputy; a new subscription was opened and measures were taken to remove the houses which cluttered the flanks of the building. Money did not come in easily. There was, indeed, the princely generosity of Sir Paul Pindar but his was a unique case. Gentry in the counties were very cool and sometimes ill demeanoured, and the Lord Mayor and Aldermen of London had to be prodded to improve their effort by a reminder that the King had promised no less than five hundred pounds a year for ten years and had taken the whole west front under his care. From Canterbury, Laud exhorted the bishops and they in turn harangued their clergy. Fines for profanity, adultery, incest and such like were diverted to the cause. But it was not an easy cause. Resentment boiled up among the citizens whose houses were pulled down. Seamen bringing stone from Portland were constantly being pressed for the navy and specific protection had to be secured for them. There was trouble at the Portland quarries, and the stone itself had to be protected from unauthorized use. On the cathedral site workmen were too often defecting. Only Laud, perhaps, could have forged his way through so much discouragement and hatred. Jones, meanwhile, set himself to produce the most refined and exact performance of his career.

What did Laud and his architect, Inigo Jones, achieve at St Paul's? Quantitatively, the accounts tell us exactly. By 1642, when the works were stopped, the whole exterior of the cathedral, except for the central tower, had been in one sense or another renewed. The fourteenth-century choir had been renewed by careful replacement of decayed masonry, including mouldings and carved ornaments. The accounts make it clear that the Gothic work was highly valued and there was no thought of modernization. With the Romanesque transepts and nave it was very different. Renewal here meant complete recasing of the exterior in Portland stone, the elevations being redesigned in the process. As for the west front, this was in part demolished and completely remodelled to become the background against which was disposed what was, in effect, a new limb of the cathedral – a gigantic Corinthian portico.

Internally, very little was done. The choir was lavishly refurnished at the expense of Sir Paul Pindar, but we have no date for this work; it is not mentioned in the accounts and was probably unconnected with Jones. Not only the choir but the Romanesque nave were left in their original condition and there is no evidence that any stylistic conversion of the nave interior was envisaged. What certainly was intended was the complete demolition of the central tower, the provision of new piers at the crossing and the building of a new tower. Of Jones's ideas for a tower we have no evidence later than the quaint proposal of 1608 [5]. There is, however, an admittedly rather speculative clue in one of John Webb's church studies. Manifestly based on Jones's ideas and teaching, it shows a structure of two stages surmounted by a *tempietto* spired by an obelisk, very much on the lines of San Gallo's twin towers for St Peter's and still with something of the profile of the *c.*1608 design.

The restored cathedral in the form in which Jones left it presents us with stylistic problems of great interest. It has usually been the practice to dismiss the recasing of the nave as a compromise in impossible conditions and to pay a cool, conventional tribute to the portico. This is wrong. It is obvious that Jones's work at St Paul's is at least as exact and subtle as anything he had previously done, both in the general conception and in the detailing of the component parts.

Consider the general conception first. We may start by bringing together the west front design of *c.* 1608 and the same front as executed in 1634–42 and preserved for us in the substantially accurate elevation drawn by Flitcroft for William Kent [43 and 44]. Leaving aside, for the moment, the portico, there are radical differences in the two treatments. Considering that they are probably twenty-five years apart one would expect no less, but the nature of the differences is instructive. The *c.* 1608 design has an arrangement of applied orders in two storeys with rustication suggested rather casually as infilling. In the executed design the only order is that of the portico; the front itself is a mass of accurately rusticated masonry uncommitted to any one of the orders. Again, the *c.* 1608 design is surmounted by an attic storey and a shaped panel with pediment between two candelabra. In the executed design all this has gone; the primitive gable shape is frankly accepted and, instead of the candelabra, we have two obelisks standing on massive pedestals. The difference between the two designs is this. In the first Jones is thinking of a pretty architectural frontispiece to hang, as it were, on the old fabric. In the second he is thinking himself into the fabric, converting the fabric itself into a powerful new design.

Look at it now more closely, relating the west front to the elevation of the clerestories and aisles [45]. The Romanesque buttresses have lent

43. St Paul's Cathedral. Design for west front, *c.*1608

44. (*Opposite*) St Paul's Cathedral. West front as executed, 1634–42

themselves to becoming broad plain pilasters going up into a plain parapet to finish with huge Roman pineapples. The pilasters of the aisles are echoed by similar pilasters in the clerestory, similarly breaking through a parapet. Across this system run two cornices: that of the clerestory, which carries across the west front and ties the whole design together, being six feet deep, the other, belonging to the aisles, rather less. Both these cornices are based on Roman 'block' cornices such as Jones had

45. St Paul's Cathedral. Detail from etching of north side by W. Hollar, 1658

used at the Queen's Chapel, St James's and perhaps at the chapel of Somerset House. Here at St Paul's his treatment makes them again appropriate. The aisle cornice seems to have been a simple adaptation of that on the precinct walls of the temple of Castor and Pollux (Palladio's 'Mars Vindicatore'), but the great upper cornice was joined with an architrave and the architrave had carved upon it lion masks alternating with sets of three vertical motifs – motifs which the accounts call 'drops', which Sir Roger Pratt was rude enough to call 'bobbins', but which in fact seem to have been inverted (as if hanging) leaf forms. This is a strange and wholly unorthodox form of decoration. It recalls Michelangelo's perversely adorned entablature in the courtyard of the Farnese, and there is certainly an association. But Jones's rhythmic arrangement is quite different; what was in his mind? The triolets of 'drops' or 'bobbins' made Pratt think of triglyphs and that may well be the answer. The 'drops' betoken triglyphs, and the masks, with which they alternate, metopes. We have here, in short, an attempt by Jones to create out of animal and vegetable motifs a kind of 'proto-Doric' or, if you prefer it, a 'quasi-Tuscan', something appropriate to the massive astylar character of his walls – appropriate also, perhaps, to the generally archaic, primitive character of the Norman nave he was enveloping. Such a deliberate quest for the primitive brings us close to the mood of Covent Garden.

Of Covent Garden, indeed, we are reminded at once when we look at the clerestory windows with their utterly plain architraves, and at the circular windows in the aisles. The great aisle windows below are a little more complicated but not much. Here the architrave is relieved by a fillet at its outer edge, while over the key-stone is the winged head of a cherub which seems to give central support to a cornice whose ends rest on consoles. This arrangement certainly comes from one of Michelangelo's windows at St Peter's but it is rigorously simplified, 'blocked-out' one might say, to suit the quasi-Tuscan mood. Of Jones's deliberate scaling-down to a robust and dour mode of expression there can be little doubt. Pratt observed it and thought it overdone – he would have been happier with sunk panels in the parapets and balustrades in the windows. We would hardly share his view. Jones, involuntarily, was looking one hundred and twenty years ahead to the dour magnificence of Newgate Prison, one of the most admired monuments of English neo-Classicism.

If we allow the recasing of the nave to be in a quasi-Tuscan mood, we must now consider the fact that in the two transept ends were lodged Ionic portals, that the north and south doors of the nave had pronounced Doric accents and, finally, that the most memorable feature of all, the west portico, was Corinthian. A cathedral is a very big thing and it may be that in his handling of St Paul's Jones deliberately thought in linked episodes within a wide range of stylistic moods – near-Tuscan for the body, Doric for the lesser doorways, Ionic for the greater and, for the grand Royal approach at the west, Corinthian.

This famous portico had a material if rather mean application to practical requirements; it was intended to harbour the mob of loiterers, touts and hucksters who made the cathedral nave their habitual rendezvous and had created the standing blasphemy of 'Paul's Walk'. A loftier and, doubtless, the real incentive was to preface the metropolitan cathedral with a royal offering of the most sumptuous kind. It was in 1634 that Charles I undertook to pay for the whole of the new west front out of his own revenue and the work was begun in October of that year. The idea of a great porch, ten columns wide, without a pediment, projecting from the end of a structure twice its height, Jones took from Palladio's reconstruction of the temple of Venus and Rome. The order, both in shape and size, he based upon that of the temple of Antoninus and Faustina, an order which, to the modern eye, is at once the least elaborated and most eloquently profiled of the Corinthian orders of Rome. Its height is 57 ft, 4½ in. That of Jones's St Paul's was 56 ft. In modular terms his columns were a trifle thicker than the Roman temple, his cornices identical, but his frieze and architrave both shallower. The intercolumniation was extraordinarily subtle. A range of columns like this, lacking the gathering effect of a pediment, has a tendency to weakness at the ends : the columns want to fall outwards. At St Paul's, Jones's solution was to give a pronouncedly greater intercolumniation to the centre bay and then to close the ends with a penultimate column standing up against a column of square section.

At the time of its erection, there was no other portico of comparable dimensions north of the Alps; and when we consider that in modern London not even the British Museum colonnade mounts to the same height it will be seen what a miraculous performance this was in the England of Charles I and what a tragedy it is that it now lives for us only in a few tiny etchings, one architectural elevation and a hasty topographical sketch. Of the rich coffered timber ceiling we know nothing; of the three marble doorways behind the portico only what we can see in Flitcroft's elevation.

Inigo Jones at sixty-one was an implacable perfectionist. The cornices and window ornaments at St Paul's were all tried out *in situ* with full-scale prototypes in timber with the cornice features modelled. Similarly the whole entablature of the west portico was erected in timber, the enrichments and inscription painted in and the statues cut out in board before a stone was cut. In the construction nothing was left to chance. John Webb who, as clerk engrosser, was on the job from beginning to end, discloses that Inigo reached an interpretation of Vitruvius' obscure passage about *scamilli impares* and had the portico set out with what he concluded to be the Roman method of optical correction. At the Portland quarries the same remorseless standards were upheld. It was only after two years quarrying that the perfect stone for the architrave at the wide central intercolumniation was extracted.

When Webb boasts that with this portico Jones 'contracted the envy of all *Christendom* upon our Nation, for a Piece of Architecture, not to be parallell'd in these last Ages of the World', he is not being silly. He is exaggerating only in that 'all Christendom' had precious little chance of seeing or even hearing of so enviable a piece. It was barely finished before civil war clashed over the cathedral, disrupting the corporate body which governed it, dispersing its property and raping its fabric. The portico, Dugdale tells us, was filled with gimcrack shops and lofts, the columns hacked to house their joists, the statues thrown down. The portico did indeed survive and, at the Restoration, could have been and doubtless would have been rendered into something near its original perfection. Then came the Fire and the ruination of the whole body of the church. Still the portico stood and there is one design by Wren for the new St Paul's which contrives to preserve it. But in the end it had to go; it was demolished in April 1687, having existed for forty-five years, but perhaps for only three or four of these in unmolested serenity.

Inigo Jones's St Paul's never received from the eighteenth century the acclaim which glorified Covent Garden. It was, of course, no longer there to be acclaimed. In any case, the recognition of its liberating innovations had already been received by a greater architectural mind than any which the eighteenth century produced – Sir Christopher Wren's. That Wren admired and envied the portico and would willingly have saved it goes without saying. That his own St Paul's owed much in its initial stages to the remodelling of its precursor is well known. Not so obvious, perhaps, is the fact that the simple, vernacular terms of many of the City churches derive from the 'quasi-Tuscan' of old St Paul's. Those trios of plain roundheaded windows, those cherub's-head key-stones, those circular holes with plain architraves, even one or two of the lantern-topped towers have their origin in the Jonesian style. Not that they do that style full justice; they merely avail themselves of its simplicity. In intention it was something more profound, reaching back to fundamental sources of the dignity and splendour of architecture in the service of religion.

Inigo at Sixty

Between the completion of St Paul's, Covent Garden, and the commence-
ment of the work at St Paul's Cathedral, Inigo Jones reached and passed
his sixtieth year. He had ruled the King's Works for eighteen years and
been the main creative agent of the masques for twenty-eight. Under him,
the Works had operated with exemplary smoothness. A critical deficit
early in his surveyorship he had ironed out by the brusque expedient of
suspending his own pay and persuading the senior officers to do the same.
The personnel of the Works under his administration had scarcely changed
and the team kept together up to the time when the whole organization
was disrupted by Parliament and Jones himself displaced.

For his personal assistant he had at this time the devoted and not un-
talented John Webb. Webb had come to him as a young man of seventeen
in 1628 and married a relative, Anne Jones. He was to be associated with
Inigo till his death, publishing his findings on Stonehenge and, at the
Restoration of 1660, forming the only consequential link between the old
court building practice and the new. But for the Civil War and its conse-
quences he would have succeeded Jones as Surveyor; indeed, he declared
that his training was directed to that end by command of the King –
Charles I thus prudently taking out an insurance against the disablement or
loss of an officer on whom so much in the visual projection of his king-
ship depended. Webb's education was immensely thorough. Not only was
he constantly involved in works in hand but was set to make thesis designs
and theoretical drawings of a kind which suggest that some kind of publication or reference collection may have been intended. More than that,
he became eventually Jones's architectural amanuensis. We shall see that all
the designs for a new Whitehall were drawn by him, the object presumably
being to plant firmly in the mind of the successor designate a project
which an architect past his sixtieth year could not hope to undertake.

The masques from 1625 to 1640 increased continually in scenic elaboration. They started with a French Pastoral, given by the Queen at Somerset House in February 1626. The scene, by Jones, showed a street with a Corinthian Temple on one side and, opposite, a prototypal classical house; elsewhere, rough peasant cottages. It seems to echo Jones's thoughts on the origins of architecture and his perennial interest in the primitive. Few of the much more ambitious scenes in the later masques are as interesting. The Roman atrium in *Albion's Triumph* (1632) is borrowed from Giulio Parigi and the amphitheatre in the same masque is a not very thoughtful adaptation of an engraving in Cesariano's edition of Vitruvius. The arbours in *Tempe Restored* (1632) are from Parigi, as is the Palace of Fame in *Britannia Triumphans* (1638). Jones seems to have thought it not worth while to create new architectural compositions for these ephemeral events; he had enough on his hands with the costumes and the mechanics of transformation scenes. He did take some trouble however with some of the proscenium borders; these seem to be original and show an extraordinary facility in the design of Mannerist ornament.

After 1631 he no longer worked with Ben Jonson. For many years Jonson had disliked Jones and been jealous of the ascendancy of spectacle over poetry – of Jones over Jonson. Inigo was perfectly conscious that it was his stage scenes and effects which were the prime source of wonder in the Whitehall audience; and when, in 1631, Jonson published the text of *Loves Triumph through Callipolis* with his name before Jones's on the title page, the latter complained furiously. And perhaps with some justice, for that masque in particular consisted of little but transformations. Ben Jonson's humiliation and hate burst out in the *Expostulation*:

O Showes! Showes! Mighty Showes!
The Eloquence of Masques! What need of prose
Or Verse, or Sense t'express Immortall you?
You are the Spectacles of State!

Indeed he was; and no poetic invention could prosper in a theatre where everything was tense with excitement about who or what was going to appear or disappear or change into something else:

> The majesty of Juno in the Cloudes,
> And peering forth of Iris in the Shrowdes!
> Th'ascent of Lady Fame which none could spy
> Not they that sided her, Dame Poetry,
> Dame History, Dame Architecture too,
> And Goody Sculpture, brought with much adoe
> To hold her up.

Jonson exposes the pantomine silliness which protrudes so embarrassingly from the Stuart masque, whatever, in the most fortunate circumstances, its excellences may have been. Later, in the *Tale of a Tub*, written or rewritten in 1633, Inigo Jones is caricatured by Jonson in the comic figure of the Islington cooper, In-and-in Medlay. But the caricature is not too vicious (the King had censored the malignant onslaught of an earlier draft) and is interesting because of the burlesqued fragments of Jonesian conversation. Medlay's companions are three wiseacres – a tinker, a farrier and a writer. Squire Tub of Totten-Court wants a masque and asks their advice. 'There stands the man can do't Sir', says Clench, the farrier, pointing to Medlay. 'But who shall write it?' asks Tub, to which Scribes, the writer replies:

> He'll do't alone Sir, He will joyne with no man,
> Though he be a Joyner: in designe he cals it,
> He must be sole Inventer: *In-and-In*
> Draws with no other in 's project, hee'll tell you,
> It cannot else be feazable, or conduce:
> These are his ruling words.

Sure enough. Medlay, asked by the squire if he can put on a masque of his own life-story, replies 'If it conduce / To the designe, what ere is feazible'. But he must survey the hall,

> For all invention, Sir,
> Comes by degrees, and on the view of nature;
> A world of things, concurre to the designe,
> Which make it feazible, if Art conduce.

Which reads (and is doubtless meant to read) like a somewhat muddled recollection of Alberti, Book IX, Chapter 5. In another passage, Jones's obsession with numbers comes clear through the burlesque. Clench praises the squire – 'a fine Gentleman!' 'He is more', says Medlay,

> A gentleman and a halfe; almost a Knight;
> Within zixe inches: that's his true measure.
>
> *
>
> I know his d'ameters, and circumference:
> A Knight is sixe diameters; and a Squire
> Is vive, and zomewhat more: I know 't by compasse,
> And skale of man.

Everything which Jonson says about Jones is designed to exhibit his egotism, his arrogance and his pedantry and an unjust fate has seen to it that such personal information as we have about Jones reflects precisely the first two of those qualities. Only Webb protests that he was neither arrogant nor ambitious, instancing his modesty in not publishing his Stonehenge results to the world. This, from his disciple, is no very striking proof of diffidence or self-criticism and we are compelled to see Jones as a personality of alarming force, totally intolerant of the lesser creatures in his environment, convinced of his indispensability to the Crown and his own indisputable authority in all that concerned building and the arts. Jonson's lampoon, *To Inigo Marquess Would Be*, suggesting that Inigo anticipated a peerage from Charles I (on the analogy of Philip IV's ennoblement of his architect, Crescenzi), is probably an exaggeration, but not entirely beside the point. Of his closeness to the King and Queen there is no doubt and one of the few intimate glimpses we have of him (through the eyes of the Papal agent accredited to Henrietta Maria) is in the company of the King, Arundel and another Lord, throwing off his cloak, fixing his glasses, expatiating on some newly arrived Italian pictures and congratulating himself repeatedly on his accuracy of attribution. 'Huomo vanissimo e molto vantatore', observes the Italian, adding that Jones, in spite of his vaunted passion for Italian art was, in fact, 'puritanissimo fiero'.

This last epithet contradicts the tradition accepted by Wren, among others, that Jones was a Roman Catholic. That he was a Puritan in the accepted sense is unlikely in the extreme and the word is probably used here to mean simply a non-Catholic intellectual. The Superior of the Queen's Capuchins, reporting to Rome on the completion of the Somerset House chapel in 1636 commented on the architect's irreligion, inferring rather curiously that Jones had been an unwilling collaborator, but admitting too that the completed chapel was 'more beautiful larger and grander than one could ever have hoped for'.

Considering the eminence of Jones at Charles I's court and how much we know of other eminences there, the relative silence of tradition as to his personality and mode of life is curious. Van Dyck's splendid drawing at Chatsworth records a countenance which is as unforgettable as Michelangelo's, but it is no use pretending that the reconstruction of personalities from portraits is anything but guesswork. Jones seems never to have married. He remains enigmatic; all we can believe in is the arrogant showmanship and the capacity for incessant work, but these we have to reconcile with the reserve, the gentleness and sensibility which inform in all his architecture.

Town and Country

Inigo Jones's responsibilities to the Crown, whether as the King's personal adviser or as head of his Works, were manifold and unremitting. He was rarely able and perhaps did not care to design buildings for private persons. Nevertheless there were those who could attract his professional attention either because of their own exalted station at court or on the score of personal friendship. There is evidence of this among the drawings. There is, for instance, a most interesting design sketched by Webb but marked by him 'Mr Surveyor', for a town house in Blackfriars for Sir Peter Killigrew [46]. Killigrew had been of service to Charles I in the Spanish marriage adventure. Charles knighted and pensioned him soon after

46. Sir Peter Killigrew's House (sketch by J. Webb)

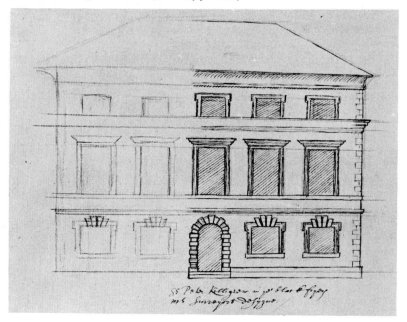

his accession, so the date of the design is likely to be in the late twenties. It was, for London, a big house with a five-window front to the street. It was also, for London, an innovating house. The ground floor was simply a compact version of a traditional English type; but it was low, and the main rooms – including dining-room, withdrawing-room and two fine bedrooms – were all on the much loftier first floor. In short, it was a small Italian *palazzo*, with a *piano nobile*. The façade – more like an Italian palace than anything in London before Barry's Reform Club of 1836 – was very much that of the Prince's Lodging at Newmarket with the centrepiece left out. Once again we are reminded of the consistency of Jones's work – of the small number of elements which he chose to combine and recombine.

In 1638 Jones designed a building for Lord Maltravers, to be built in Lothbury. Maltravers was the thirty-year-old son of Jones's great patron and friend, Lord Arundel, and he had obtained from the King a patent to coin royal farthing tokens. For the change and issue of these tokens he established an office on the family property in Lothbury and of the two designs which we have for it, one, with a six-column portico, has a decidedly official character. The other, more modest [47], is closely related to the Covent Garden houses, though of course without the arcades. But what makes this modest elevation of very special interest is its connexion with a design for a terrace of four large houses, fenestrated exactly as the house but with an additional storey [48]. Most probably this represents a scheme for developing the Arundel land in Lothbury and it is the first instance we have (Covent Garden apart) of a row of London houses designed in a regular classical manner.

This question of regularity in London street architecture much concerned Jones. He had initiated it at Covent Garden and there cannot be much doubt that the uniformity of, at least, the west side of Lincoln's Inn Fields was due to the exercise of his authority. As built from 1638 onwards,

47. Design for Lord Maltravers, Lothbury, London, 1638

48. Design for houses, probably on the Arundel estate, Lothbury, c.1638

49. Lindsey House (Nos. 59 and 60), Lincoln's Inn Fields, *c.*1638–40

it consisted of more or less identical houses with three rather taller houses somewhere a little north of the middle. This was not a very artistic arrangement but the whole thing was a commercial speculation on a considerably less respectable level than Covent Garden. Of the three taller houses the centre one was the tallest and most ornamented. It still exists (as Nos. 59 and 60 Lincoln's Inn Fields) and is called Lindsey House [49]. We cannot be absolutely sure that it is by Jones, but behind its rather coarse execution is a scheme which fits exactly into the pattern of his ideas. Here again is the *piano nobile* over a low ground floor, but this time the ground floor is made the rusticated podium of an Ionic order rising through two storeys to the entablature. The first-floor windows are pedimented and the centre window has a Mannerist variation recalling the gateway to Arundel House. Lindsey House has been much altered, the lowering of most of the window-sills ruining its proportions, but the print in *Vitruvius Britannicus* shows it as designed, or nearly so. It has a forecourt with two massive rubbed brick piers capped by stone vases, recalling the stone piers of the River Stairs at Somerset House; these, however, must belong near the end of the century.

It was here, at Lincoln's Inn Fields and in near-by Great Queen Street, that Jones's influence penetrated the London vernacular. Lindsey House is recognizably 'proto-Georgian', the conscious model for some and the unacknowledged dictator of whole streets of houses in innumerable cities of the English-speaking world.

Country houses by Inigo Jones are and always were extremely rare – so rare, in fact, that not a single house can be named as being or having been indisputably his personal work. Even Wilton, whose celebrity depends so largely on its association with Jones, has recently been shown to have been built from designs by Isaac de Caux, employed on Jones's recommendation and receiving in its execution his 'advice and approbation'. One glance at the famous south front of Wilton [50], built for the Earl of

50. Wilton House, Wiltshire, south front, 1633–40

51. Wilton House, Wiltshire, the Double Cube room, c.1649

Pembroke about 1633-40, shows how closely its ratios and details are influenced by earlier Jonesian works; while the central window with its carved figures is the Scamozzi theme which he had used in the Queen's Chapel, St James's, and was to use again in his Whitehall designs. The presence of a double-cube chamber behind this great window is almost predictable; the only surprise is that it lies not back from the window but across the axis, the window penetrating the middle of one of the room's long sides. It is a room of great splendour [51] of exactly the dimensions of the Somerset House chapel. It is not, however, the room belonging to the original building. This was destroyed or badly damaged by fire in 1647 or 1648 and, although rebuilt 'with the advice of' Jones – then over seventy – has not quite the elegance of detail which he could have contributed in earlier years. The great doorways, to be sure, are versions of his Banqueting House doorway design of 1619 [17] but generally speaking the enrichments show less of the taste of Jones than of John Webb and of French designers like Jean Barbet, whose work gained much favour at the Court of Henrietta Maria. Gorgeous as the Double Cube Room is, with its Van Dycks and the cove painted by Edward Pearce, it is not a place in which one captures the essential qualities of the man who was, after all, only rather remotely its architect.

Then there are the twin pavilions and colonnades at Stoke Bruerne, Northants [52] – all that is left of the house begun (but never finished) by Sir Francis Crane, the man who established the Mortlake tapestry factory. We are told that Crane 'brought the design from Italy, and in the execution of it received the assistance of Inigo Jones'. The design [53] was doubtless rooted in the curved colonnades and pavilions of Vignola's Villa Papa Giulio, here paraphrased with much grace in a combination of lime-stone, iron-stone, stucco and wood.

For the rest, we can only faintly reconstruct what Jones built for the thirteenth Lord Dacre at Chevening before 1630 – a massive three-storey

52. Stoke Bruerne, Northamptonshire, *c*.1629–35, east pavilion

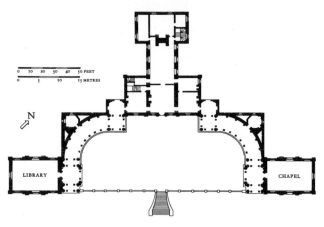

53. Stoke Bruerne, Northamptonshire, c.1629–35

mansion, seven windows wide, crowned by a Roman block-cornice. We
can puzzle over what may or may not be Jones in the plan, the classical
centrepiece (Newmarket again), and gables at Raynham, Norfolk. And we
can consider the design for a lodge made for a Mr Penruddock, presumably
John Penruddock who had an estate at Hale in Hampshire. This latter design [54], which may or may not have been executed, is dated 1638. It is
a miniature countrified version of the Queen's House at Greenwich, the
Ionic order of the upper storey being rendered into a voluted equivalent of
the bucolic Tuscan.

Another design dated 1638 brings us back to London and the Strand.
The City of London approached Jones for a design for a structure at
Temple Bar where the jurisdiction of the City and that of Westminster met.
The boundary was then probably marked only by posts and rails or chains.
Jones produced a Triumphal Arch [55]. Thinking perhaps of the Roman
scale of his St Paul's portico half a mile to the east he adopted a scale
approaching that of the Roman arches, with a total width of sixty feet and a
total height of the same. It is difficult to see how a structure of this width
could be intruded in the narrow Strand and it was, of course, never built.

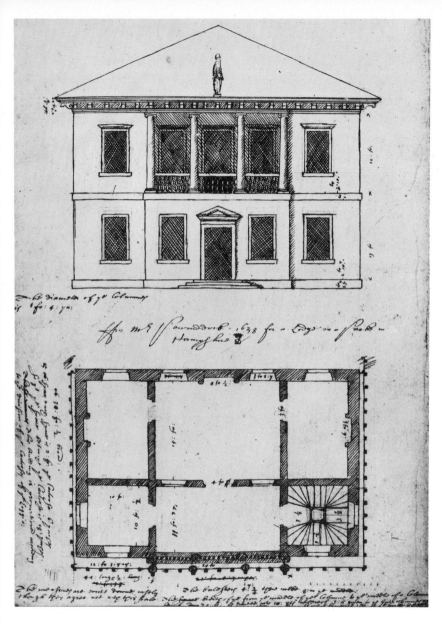

54. Design for Mr Penruddock, 1638

But the design is remarkable. The obvious models – the arches of Septimius Severus and Constantine – are wider than they are high. Jones's elevation, comprising the same elements, is an exact square, divided by the main cornice in the ratio 3 : 2, the upper part thus becoming an attic storey of abnormal height. It is, however, exactly the dimension of the twenty-four foot Composite columns below, and further subdivisions bring the whole thing into harmony.

55. (*Opposite*) Design for Temple Bar, London, 1638

56. Design for screen for Winchester Cathedral, *c.*1638

For Winchester Cathedral, in or about the same year, Jones designed a choir screen and his sensitive outline drawing survives in the Burlington–Devonshire collection [56]. It is closely related to elements in the St Paul's west front design of just thirty years before – so closely that Jones must have been conscious of executing, as it were, a critique of that product of his architectural adolescence. The screen is no longer in position, but many of its stones survive – unhappily divided between the crypt of the Cathedral and the Museum of Archaeology at Cambridge; while statues of James I and Charles I, made by Le Sueur for the niches, stand in the Cathedral nave.

If evidence were needed that in 1638, at the age of sixty-five, Jones could express himself easily and accurately at his drawing table, the designs for Temple Bar and the Winchester screen supply it. Yet a project which, just at this time, must have filled his mind almost to the exclusion of all else is one of which we possess not a single sketch. This was the tremendous plan for a new Whitehall.

The Whitehall Designs

That Charles I seriously intended to pull down the whole of the Tudor palace of Whitehall and replace it in every item of its multitudinous functions by a new, symmetrical and monumental structure is not, on the face of it, easy to believe. To us, the 1630s are overshadowed by the turmoil and disasters of the 1640s. To people living then they were not and to Charles I the consolidation of a labyrinth of out-dated, inconvenient and mostly rather poor accommodation into a single rational unit may have seemed sensible and far-sighted; perhaps even an indestructible guarantee of the sovereign values which the house of Stuart embodied. In any case the intention was there and continued to be there so long as the King lived; and even after that, for it was cherished by his son and the notion of a new Palace of Whitehall only died with the seventeenth century.

There is not, to be sure, much evidence. We do not know when the idea was first advanced or even the date of the earliest designs. Nothing in the way of correspondence or schedules of accommodation has survived – only a few oblique references and a mass of drawings. These drawings – about seventy in all, distributed between Worcester College, Oxford, Chatsworth and the British Museum – are themselves fraught with doubt and frustration and have an uneasy history. They include not one but several schemes, not all by the same hand and obviously of different dates. In the eighteenth century two of these schemes were published over Inigo Jones's name; and it was not till 1912 that anybody took seriously the fact that no drawing in any of the sets exhibits Jones's handwriting or personal draughtsmanship. Many of them were then found to be in Webb's hand and Jones's responsibility for the project receded for a time into the background. In 1946, however, there was another turn of the wheel. Dr Margaret Whinney restudied and carefully grouped the drawings in a convincing chronological order and in relation to some new scraps of historical evidence. It then became evident that two alternative schemes could plausibl y be dated in the late 1630s. The earlier of the two appeared to be for a palace in St James's Park, the later (which incorporated the Banqueting House) for a new palace to replace the old along the Thames.

These two schemes are very closely related to each other and contain, in fact, some almost identical elements. Both seem to be drawn by Webb. And yet there is a profound difference. In the first scheme every detail is so fully in accord with what we know of Jones's style and ideas in the 1630s that it could be by nobody but him. In the second, the aim of the design has shifted; there is an ambition to generalize loftily and in its pursuit has been lost what matters so much in Jones – precision of contrast and delicacy of articulation. The degree of participation of Jones in the second scheme could be argued both ways at great length. Suffice to say that the view offered here is that *only* the scheme which Dr Whinney describes as 'preparatory' is authentic Jones and that the second is a recasting both in plan and detail by somebody else, presumably Webb, somebody who is moving away from Jonesian ideas. Only the Preparatory scheme [57] will be discussed here.

The conception is of a single rectangular mass filling a great deal of St James's Park. Its main frontage is about the length of the river front of the present Houses of Parliament and its flanks even longer. It would have been more than double the size of the Escorial – a building probably not without a certain influence. Jones had never built anything one twentieth the size of this, but his approach was entirely consistent with all that had gone before. No new attitude emerges. He envisaged the new palace as a Roman patrician house on the grandest possible scale, and Palladio and Scamozzi were, as so often before, his authorities. Palladio, in his second book, deals with the Roman house, its halls and atria. Scamozzi restates some of Palladio's ideas and expands them, giving a design for a palace on the Roman model. This design is the genesis of Jones's Whitehall. But it

57. Design for Whitehall Palace, *c*.1638, block plan

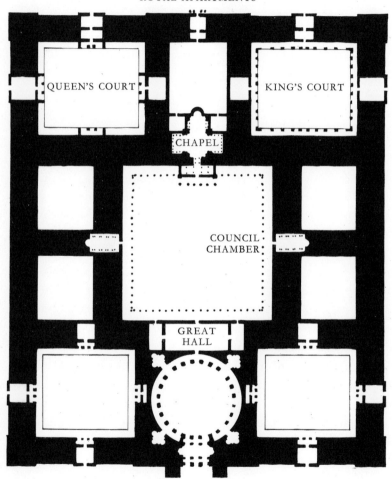

ROYAL APARTMENTS

QUEEN'S COURT

KING'S COURT

CHAPEL

COUNCIL
CHAMBER

GREAT
HALL

RIVER FRONT

0   100   200   300   400   500   600   700 FEET

58. Design for Strand front of Somerset House, 1638 (drawing by Webb)

59. Design for Whitehall Palace, c.1638, river front (drawing by Webb)

had to be developed to the necessary size, and this Jones did by the multiplication of courts within the overall rectangle. The Escorial has, in principle, eleven courts: so has Jones's palace. There is a three-hundred-foot-square central atrium and around it are ten other courts, one of them circular. There are no circular courts in either Palladio or Scamozzi or, for that matter, in the Escorial; but Pliny, describing his villa at Laurentinum mentions the *porticus* 'shaped like the letter O' through which the main court or *cavaedium* of the house was approached. Jones's circular court occupies an equivalent position.

On the far side of the main court from the entrance is the chapel (the great church of the Escorial is similarly placed), a cruciform domed building. On the right is the Council Chamber, an apsed hall reminiscent of the abandoned Star Chamber of 1616. The King's court and the Queen's court are distinguished by the highly unusual feature of porticos consisting not of columns but of human figures: male figures below supporting a Doric entablature, females above supporting a Corinthian [63]. One is reminded of Pierre Lescot's figures in the Salle des Cariatides at the Louvre.

The Louvre, indeed, was a model which in other respects than this Jones could hardly ignore for, without consulting the French method of articulating a large plan into pavilions and connecting elements, he would have been impelled by the sheer size of the scheme into devastating monotony. The Whitehall designs are well articulated within a system of pavilions and towers, though apart from this principle the elevations are scarcely French. Each element retains a strictly Jonesian character and it is never far from the antique – a temple front, a triumphal arch or the arcaded tiers of a theatre. Only in the charming elevation of the Park Front [60], in which the triumphal arch pattern is employed in two and three storeys, does there seem to be an echo of Lescot's elevations in the great court of

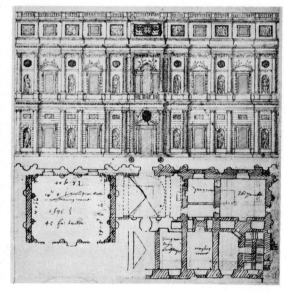

60. Design for Whitehall Palace, c.1638, detail of park front

61. Design for Whitehall Palace, c.1638, section through Great Hall

62. (*Opposite*) Design for Whitehall Palace, c.1638, plan and sections of Chapel

the Louvre; and it is a faint echo. The originality of the design in the context of European architecture of the period is, if not spectacular, definite.

Whether, had it been realized, this prodigious structure would have been an architectural triumph is an intriguing question. Given a large ambience of park – larger than the hemmed-in St James's Park of today – and given the razing of the old palace so that the new should enjoy freedom towards the Thames, one can conceive it as some kind of ideal city, an insulated New Jerusalem, opposing its sublime symmetries to the Boeotian sprawl of London and Westminster; not a walled inward-looking city but one with a fixed and formidable stare to north, south,

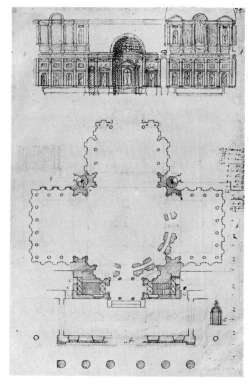

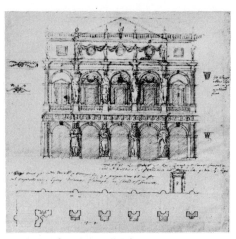

63. Design for Whitehall Palace, c.1638,
project for the Queen's Court

east and west (the Escorial again). There is little of projection or recession
in those long façades. Richly varied in sunshine, in half-light they would
spell unmitigated gloom. Penetrated, the city would be a model Rome. In
majestic succession would come the vaulted vestibule, the circular court,
a hall scarcely inferior to that of Caracalla [61] and then the square court,
colonnaded like a forum; beyond this the dome of the chapel [62]. Read
all this in the spirit of the Banqueting House and you have something of
the experience which Jones's Whitehall would have afforded. Remember
the Roman scale of the portico he built at St Paul's and you will understand the degree of affirmation at which he aimed. Akin to what Philip II
achieved at the Escorial, it would have been for Louis XIV to excel if he
could. Had Charles I lived to build it, the new Whitehall would have been
a grave and fitting backcloth for the bloodier revolution which it would
most certainly have helped to precipitate.

The Last Years

The last masque at Whitehall was *Salmacida Spolia*, written by Sir William Davenant. It was performed on 21 January and repeated on Shrove Tuesday 1640, not in the Banqueting House but in a timber building of identical proportions built to the east of it in 1637–8, expressly for the performance of masques and to avoid damage to the Rubens ceiling. *Salmacida Spolia* is a curious piece. In the circumstances of 1640 it seems designed as a dramatic incantation, willing quiescence to a nation with a troubled heart. It begins with a scene of storm and stress, passes to a serene landscape, thence to an Alpine pass representing the difficult road to the Throne of Honour. The King is invited to take this road and is shortly disclosed sitting on the throne attended by lords and by statues of ancient heroes. He is praised for the kingly wisdom, patience and courage with which he has overcome discord. Then, from the spangled shrouds of an evening sky the Queen and her ladies descend. The masque concludes with a transformation which was acknowledged as one of Inigo Jones's greatest triumphs:

Their Majesties being seated under the State, the scene was changed into magnificent buildings composed of several selected pieces of architecture: in the furthest part was a bridge over a river, where many people, coaches, horses, and such like were seen to pass to and fro: beyond this, on the shore were buildings in prospective, which shooting far from the eye shewed as the suburbs of a great city.

From the highest part of the heavens came forth a cloud far in the scene, in which were eight persons richly attired representing the spheres; this, joining with two other clouds which appear'd at that instant full of music, covered all the upper part of the scene, and, at that instant beyond all these, a heaven opened full of deities, which celestial prospect with the chorus below filled all the whole scene with apparitions and harmony.

That was the end. There were no more masques. The great spectacles of 1641 were the trial and execution of the Earl of Strafford.

Inigo Jones suddenly found himself in the full beam of Puritan hate. As the conductor of ruinously expensive court entertainments, as the executive of arbitrary proclamations about London building and, most especially, as the accomplice of Archbishop Laud he was marked for trouble. In December 1641 he was made to appear before the House of Lords to answer a charge brought by the parishioners of St Gregory's, a church whose fabric adjoined the south-west corner of St Paul's. The charge was to the effect that he had demolished part of their church and threatened that if they did not take down the rest it would be thrown into the street and the parishioners 'laid by the heels'. The autocrat of the arts, the 'Sole Monarch' (as the charge ironically described him) of the St Paul's works, offered a procrastinating defence. He was not impeached, but the parishioners were appeased and allowed to mend their church.

In January 1642 the King left Whitehall for the north, making his headquarters at York. In April he attempted to enter Hull but was refused. Three months later he made Beverley his base for a formal siege of the place. Inigo Jones was there, probably for the obvious reason that the Surveyor of Works would be expected to be as wise in fortification and siege warfare as in architecture (two of Jones's recent predecessors, Basil and Adams, had both been fortification specialists). That he had studied fortification we know from his annotations of Lorini, but he can never have done any campaigning. At Hull, the siege was not pressed and it was at Nottingham, on 22 August, that Charles I raised his standard.

For three years after that date we know nothing of Jones's movements. He would certainly be with the King at Oxford. In London, before 1 June 1644, Parliament reorganized the Royal Works, installing a usurping surveyor in the person of Edward Carter, who had been Jones's executive at St Paul's. Also in London, John Webb, now Jones's deputy, employed himself making stealthy plans of the Parliamentary fortifications and sending them to the King. In October 1645, we find Jones involved in the sack of Basing House. We know from a Parliamentary news-sheet that he was 'gotten thither for help to the House', probably in the period between the raising of the twenty-four weeks' siege in November 1644 and the final assault by Cromwell nearly a year later. The same source describes Jones as 'an excellent architector to build, but no engineer to pull down' which suggests that he failed to demolish the siege works raised around Basing by the Parliamentary forces. The capture of Inigo Jones, 'the famous Surveyer and great Enemy of St Grigory', and 'contriver of scenes for the Queen's Dancing Barne' gave lively pleasure in the enemy camp, one chronicler adding that 'he was carried away in a blanket, having lost his cloaths'. He had probably been stripped by one of Cromwell's troopers.

He was lucky to be alive. The sequestration of his estate followed, but an application to the Committee for Compounding resulted in the settlement of the affair on payment of a fine and a sum of £500 representing his 'fifth and twentieth part'. In July 1646 his pardon was confirmed by the Lords and his estate restored. Of his life during the next two years we know nothing, but we do know that at Hampton Court and later at Carisbrooke, Charles I still dreamed of a new Whitehall and had Webb submit fresh plans to him.

Charles was executed on 30 January 1649. Later in that year Jones and Webb were providing designs for new work for the Earl of Pembroke at Wilton. On 22 July 1650 Jones made his will. On 21 June 1652 he died, 'through grief, as is well known', says Webb, 'for the fatal calamity of his dread master'. He died, however, neither poor nor oppressed. He evidently had lodgings at Somerset House and was able to leave a moderate fortune.

He was buried with his parents in the church of St Benet Paul's Wharf, and a monument for which he had provided in his will was raised there. It consisted of a pedestal with a carved bust and representations in relief of the portico of St Paul's Cathedral and another of his works (according to one source the Covent Garden church, according to another the Banqueting House). The monument was destroyed with the church in the Great Fire of 1666.

John Webb inherited a substantial part of the fortune and bought himself an estate in Somerset. He also inherited the drawings. These, in due course, he left to his son with instructions that they should not be dispersed. The son's widow, however, sold some of them to Dr Clarke of Oxford. Others passed through various hands till they came into those of Lord Burlington. Others again were lost. Dr Clarke left his share to Worcester College, Oxford, while Lord Burlington's passed by inheritance into the Chatsworth collection. Today nearly all the known surviving drawings are either at Worcester College, at Chatsworth or in the Burlington–Devonshire collection (deriving from Chatsworth) at the Royal Institute of British Architects.

These drawings and an ever-diminishing number of buildings have borne the reputation of Inigo Jones through three centuries. In one of these centuries, the eighteenth, his authority became such as, perhaps, only he, with his enormous egotism and unbounded assurance could fail to find astonishing. He was called the British Vitruvius and the modern counterpart of Palladio; his works were engraved in sumptuous volumes and copied into practical handbooks; his bust or his profile became symbols of high learning in libraries and galleries: more than that, English architecture bowed to his conception of architectural truth. It is not only, or indeed chiefly, to Palladio that the Palladianism of our eighteenth century is indebted; it is first and foremost to Jones and to his revaluation of a tradition.

Jones saw certain things clearly – more clearly than his Italian and French contemporaries with their immensely richer and more sophisticated backgrounds could do. He saw that antiquity offered, in the five orders and in their attachment to specific forms of spatial arrangement, a language of timeless validity. This the Italians had known and still knew, but had dissipated in dominant conventions of their own. Jones saw it, through the eyes of Vitruvius and the Renaissance theorists, with fresh intensity and confirmed it in the course of his own Italian travels. He appreciated the inventions of Mannerism but subordinated them always to Rome and to rational procedure. 'Solid, proportionable according to the rules, masculine and unaffected' is the phrase in which he perfectly described the precision and moderation of his approach. His was not the spirit of revolution; but such was the force of his example that, sustained through two generations of eclectic experiment and Baroque adventure, it showed the way, in a new age, to a new enlightenment.

Bibliography

The following are the more significant books and papers relating to Inigo Jones, his life and works. They are listed chronologically by date of publication.

SEVENTEENTH CENTURY

J. Webb, *The Most notable Antiquity called Stone-Heng*, 1655. Based on notes by Inigo Jones and containing some biographical passages.

J. Webb, *A Vindication of Stone-Heng Restored*, 1665 (2nd ed., 1725). Contains a few further biographical notes.

EIGHTEENTH CENTURY

C. Campbell, *Vitruvius Britannicus*, 3 vols. 1715–25. This book, containing many plans and elevations of buildings by Jones, inaugurated the revival of interest in his work.

'Memoirs relating to the Life and Writings of Inigo Jones Esq.', prefixed to the 1725 edition of John Webb, *Stone-Heng Restored*.

W. Kent, *Designs of Inigo Jones, with some additional Designs*, 2 vols., 1727. Engraved from drawings by Henry Flitcroft based on the Inigo Jones designs acquired by Lord Burlington.

I. Ware, *Designs of Inigo Jones and Others*, 1735 (?). A slight work, supplementing the last.

J. Vardy, *Some Designs of Mr. Inigo Jones and Mr. William Kent*, 1744. Another addendum to Kent.

Biographica Britannica, Vol. IV, 1757. Article on Jones, pp. 2770–5.

H. Walpole, *Anecdotes of Painting in England,* 5 vols., 1762–71. The account of Inigo Jones is in Vol. II, pp. 142–54.

F. Milizia, *Le Vite de' piu celebri Architetti d'ogni Nazione*, Rome, 1768. Life of Jones, pp. 330–4. Ill-informed but appreciative. The book was translated and revised by Eliza (Mrs Edward) Cresy and published in 1826, with a dedication to Soane.

A. Cunningham, *The Lives of . . . British Painters, Sculptors and Architects*, 6 vols., 1829–33. The life of Jones occurs in Vol. IV (1831), pp. 70–146. Dedicated to Soane. An advance on previous lives.

P. Cunningham, *Inigo Jones: a Life of the Architect*, with *Remarks on some of his Sketches for Masques* by J. R. Planché and *Five Court Masques*, ed. J. Payne Collier. (Shakespeare Society), 1848–9, re-issued 1853. The first really scholarly biography.

Architectural Publication Society, *The Dictionary of Architecture*, Vol. III, *c.* 1868. Article on Inigo Jones, pp. 22–6 (by Wyatt Papworth). Interesting for the extensive lists of attributed works.

R. T. Blomfield, articles on Inigo Jones in *The Portfolio*, 1889, pp. 88, 113, 126.

A. P. Horne. The unsigned article, 'Inigo Jones', in the *Dictionary of National Biography* (1891–2) is based on Horne's MS notes. Valuable for the many references to primary sources. Horne also wrote on Jones in his periodical, the *Hobby-horse*, 1893, etc.

W. J. Loftie, *Inigo Jones and Wren* or *The Rise and Decline of Modern Architecture in England*, 1893. Vague and tendentious.

R. T. Blomfield, *A History of Renaissance Architecture in England, 1500–1800*, 2 vols., 1897. Chapter 5, Vol 1, on Inigo Jones. Acknowledges the liberal assistance of A. P. Horne (see above).

A. Clark (ed.), *'Brief Lives' . . . by John Aubrey*, 1898, Vol. II, p. 10. The section on Jones contains little more than some notes on his monument and on the construction of the James I catafalque.

TWENTIETH CENTURY

H. Inigo Triggs and H. Tanner, *Some Architectural Works of Inigo Jones*, 1901. A folio of measured drawings of buildings mostly not by Inigo Jones.

W. R. Lethaby, 'Inigo Jones and the Theatre', *Architectural Review*, April 1912.

J. A. Gotch, 'The Original Drawings for the Palace at Whitehall, attributed to Inigo Jones', *Architectural Review*, June 1912.

W. G. Keith, 'Some Hitherto Unknown Drawings by Inigo Jones', *Burlington Magazine*, XXII, January 1913.

W. G. Keith, 'The Palace of Oatlands', *Architectural Review*, XXXIX, 1916.

W. R. Lethaby, 'New Light on Inigo Jones', *Architectural Review*, XL, 1916.

M. Hervey, *Life of Thomas Howard, Earl of Arundel*, 1921. Important for the account of Arundel's Italian journey with Jones.

S. C. Ramsey, *Inigo Jones*, 1924. Short essay with photographs.

P. Simpson and C. F. Bell, *Designs by Inigo Jones for Masques and Plays at Court*, Walpole Society, Vol. XII, 1924. Complete catalogue with fifty-one plates.

J. A. Gotch, 'Inigo Jones, some Surviving Misconceptions', *R.I.B.A. Journal*, 3rd ser., XXXI, 1924.

W. G. Keith, 'Inigo Jones as a Collector', *R.I.B.A. Journal*, 3rd ser., XXXIII 1925–6.

J. A. Gotch, *Inigo Jones*, 1928. Based largely on P. Cunningham and A. P. Horne with a few new facts. Adequate, in spite of the wilfully 'readable' style.

G. H. Chettle, *The Queen's House, Greenwich*, London Survey monograph, 1937.

W. G. Keith, 'The Queen's House, Greenwich', *R.I.B.A. Journal*, 3rd ser., XLIV, 1937. A critique of the last.

A. Nicoll, *Stuart Masques and the Renaissance Stage*, 1937.

G. H. Chettle, 'Marlborough House Chapel', *Country Life*, 5 November 1938.

E. V. Mikhailovskii, *Arkhitektor Inigo Dzhons*, U.S.S.R. Academy of Architecture, 1939.

E. S. De Beer, 'Notes on Inigo Jones', *Notes and Queries*, 30 December 1939 and 4 May 1940.

'Inigo Jones and St Paul's Cathedral', *London Topographical Record*, XVIII, 1942.

M. Whinney, *John Webb's Drawings for Whitehall Palace*, Walpole Society, Vol. XXXI, 1946. A basic study of the drawings representing Jones's designs.

C. Rowe, *The Theoretical Drawings of Inigo Jones, their Sources and Scope*, University of London thesis, 1947.

R. Wittkower, 'Puritanissimo Fiero', *Burlington Magazine*, XC, 1948.

M. Whinney, 'Inigo Jones: a Revaluation', *R.I.B.A. Journal*, 3rd ser., LIX, 1952.

J. Summerson, *Architecture in Britain 1530–1830*, 1953 (4th ed., 1963), chapters 7, 8 and 9 on Inigo Jones.

R. Wittkower, 'Inigo Jones, Architect and Man of Letters', *R.I.B.A. Journal*, LX, January 1953.

J. Lees-Milne, *The Age of Inigo Jones*, 1953

H. M. Colvin, 'The South Front of Wilton House', *Archaeological Journal*, CXI, 1954.

P. Palme, *Triumph of Peace; a study of the Whitehall Banqueting House*, Stockholm, 1956.

J. Harris, 'Inigo Jones and the Prince's Lodging at Newmarket', *Architectural History*, Vol. II, 1959.

L. Stone, 'Inigo Jones and the New Exchange', *Archaeological Journal*, CXIV, 1959.

R.I.B.A., *Catalogue of the drawings by Inigo Jones . . . in the Burlington–Devonshire Collection* (typescript), 1960.

J. Summerson 'Inigo Jones' (British Academy 'Master Mind' lecture), *Proc. of the British Academy*, Vol. L, 1965. A detailed consideration of Covent Garden and the restoration of St Paul's.

Index

More about Penguins
and Pelicans

If you have enjoyed reading this book you may wish to know that *Penguin Book News* appears every month. It is an attractively illustrated magazine containing a complete list of books published by Penguins and still in print, together with details of the month's new books. A specimen copy will be sent free on request.

Penguin Book News is obtainable from most bookshops; but you may prefer to become a regular subscriber at 3s. for twelve issues. Just write to Dept EP, Penguin Books Ltd, Harmondsworth, Middlesex, enclosing a cheque or postal order, and you will be put on the mailing list.

Some other books published by Penguins are described on the following pages.

Note: *Penguin Book News* is not available in the U.S.A., Canada or Australia

Victorian Architecture

Robert Furneaux Jordan

We are still in the Victorian age – the iron train sheds, the smoke-blackened monuments of the North, the shades of Gothic in churches, palaces, and surburban streets, the grim terraces of mining towns . . . these form a backdrop to our world. In Victorian architecture are expressed the triumphs, contradictions, and failures of Victorian society. This book encourages us to understand what, as we look around, we cannot ignore.

Bernini

Howard Hibbard

Gianlorenzo Bernini was the greatest sculptor and one of the greatest architects of the seventeenth century. Today his work is everywhere in evidence in Rome – in the design of the colonnaded *piazza* before St Peter's, in a sequence of magnificent Baroque fountains, in lavish and fantastic decorative enterprises within St Peter's itself, and in a number of portrait busts and mythological and religious sculptures of unrivalled technical perfection and dramatic power. Bernini served Louis XIV as well as a succession of popes. His work expresses the spirit of his age perhaps more than that of any other artist in history.

In this new study Howard Hibbard reveals the gradual evolution of a revolutionary artistic vision which embraced painting, sculpture, and architecture and ultimately merged them into one dramatic whole. Whilst the biographical aspect of *Bernini* must have an interest for any reader, the student will find that this lavishly illustrated book makes an important contribution to our understanding of the age of Baroque and of one of its greatest artists.

French Architecture

Pierre Lavedan

This book, of which the French version has run into many editions, is a history of French architecture from its origins until the present day. This Pelican edition represents its first appearance in English. Unlike many writers on architecture, Professor Lavedan does not subjugate the problems of technique and materials to aesthetic considerations. He sees that almost every major architectural innovation has resulted equally from technical and artistic demands. For this reason the first chapter of the book provides a general account of the materials and technique of building, which is not readily available in such a compact form elsewhere. The first part of the book also discusses the important question of 'style'. The rest is in the main divided into two sections dealing respectively with the history of religious and civil architecture from medieval times until the present. In addition there are chapters on town-planning and the planning of gardens, biographies of the chief architects discussed, a bibliography, and the book is illustrated with line drawings in the text and sixty-four pages of plates.

The Gothic Revival

Kenneth Clark

Few movements in the history of art and taste have been so derided as the Gothic Revival. In this lively study – a new edition of his first book – Sir Kenneth Clark examines the Gothic Revival with highly critical sympathy. He traces the neo-Gothic impulse from its origins in eighteenth-century literature through the pseudo-medieval houses and follies to the Oxford Movement, Gilbert Scott, and Ruskin, all of whom receive detailed attention.

He reminds us of the movement's successes as well as its notorious failures. If Walpole's Strawberry Hill is mere quaintness, and if many of Scott's church restorations were indefensible, the Gothic Revival did produce Pugin, Butterfield, and Street, and would be remembered by every visitor to London for the Houses of Parliament alone.

'Sympathetic but discerning treatment of a mainly English phenomenon' – *The Times Literary Supplement*

'A new edition of his 34-year-old classic, still unrivalled' – Philip Rawson in the *Sunday Telegraph*

An Outline of
European Architecture

Nikolaus Pevsner

This seventh revised edition of Nikolaus Pevsner's classic
history is presented in an entirely new and attractive style. The
format has been enlarged and the illustrations appear next to the
passages to which they refer. Their numbers have swelled to
nearly 300, including drawings, plans, and photographs. The
final chapter of the Penguin Jubilee edition (published in 1960
and still available at £7 7s) has been incorporated, carrying the
story from 1914 to the present day, and there are substantial
additions on the sixteenth to eighteenth centuries in France as
well as many minor revisions. The book tells the story of
architecture by concentrating on outstanding buildings, and
reads exceedingly well in its concentration and its combination
of warmth and scholarship.

An Introduction to
Modern Architecture

J. M. Richards

'It has never been more important for the ordinary man to pick out what is bogus in modern architecture, and Mr Richards is a master at explaining architecture in simple language' – *The Times Literary Supplement*

An Introduction to Modern Architecture, which has been newly revised and brought up to date, sets out to explain what 'modern' architecture is all about. With the help of gravure illustrations, as well as line drawings, it explains how modern buildings come to look as they do, discussing the technical practices and the changing needs and ideals on which modern arachitects' work is based. Also, believing that architecture can only be explained as part of a continuous growth, he shows modern architecture against the background out of which it grew, giving an outline history of the struggle to produce a sane architecture which has been going on throughout the past hundred years.

another Pelican by

John Summerson

Georgian London

George I came to the throne in 1714; George IV died in 1830. Between those dates Georgian London transformed itself into a great Imperial Capital. A criss-cross pattern of streets and squares covered former marshes and meadows; new bridges spanned the Thames at Westminster and Blackfriars, and later at three more points; new roads linked Paddington and Islington, and pushed down into Southwark and Lambeth; villages such as Hackney and Fulham became suburbs; and the arcaded terraces of Somerset House and the Adelphi hinted at a Thames Embankment. These are some of the bare facts of the development: in *Georgian London* Sir John Summerson fills them with life and meaning, showing how closely the buildings and the history of an age are connected. Statesmen, connoisseurs, merchants, architects, and jerrybuilders – all are characters in this absorbing story.

'The title gives no idea of the variety and scope, the interest and entertainment, of this learned and lively book. It treats not only of Georgian architecture, but of the whole problem of the growth of a city' – *The Times Literary Supplement*

a further volume in the Penguin series
The Architect and Society

James S. Ackerman

Palladio

Palladio is the most imitated architect in history. His buildings have been copied all over the Western world – from Leningrad to Philadelphia – and his ideas on proportion are still current nearly four hundred years after his death. In this, the first full account of his career to be published in English, Professor James Ackerman investigates the reasons for his enormous and enduring success. He presents him in his historical setting as the contemporary of Titian, Tintoretto, and Veronese, but is constantly alert to his relevance for us today.